In Her Garden, Encroaching On The Iris

In Her Garden, Encroaching On The Iris

Angela Menking

Pentland Press, Inc.
England·USA·Scotland

PUBLISHED BY PENTLAND PRESS, INC.
5122 Bur Oak Circle, Raleigh, North Carolina 27612
United States of America
(919)782-0281

ISBN: 1-57197-104-1
Library of Congress Catalog Card Number 97-075988
Copyright © 1998 Angela Menking
Printed in the United States of America

to the children of the Blue Ray

Table of Contents

Preface

The iris is related to healing, purity and immortality. A perennial with sword-shaped leaves, the iris is a border plant whose soft stem dies down to the ground after flowering. When we encroach on the iris, and cross the border into her garden, we may feel suddenly dizzy and in chaos, beclouded. But if we remain still and receptive, a concrescence of gifts is placed before us. A great flowering of art, language, philosophy, science and architecture springs forth. A renaissance. We now recognize within ourselves a cupboard of wild beauty.

Acknowledgements

I deeply thank these people who were exceptionally enthu-siastic, giving in time, and helpful in feedback on this manuscript. Thank you, Marc, for being married to me. You are the other author/visionary of this book. We have never had a boring conversation. You are the one I adore. Thank you Susan, my ebullient mom, for your liberal arts sensibility, your caring and belief. And thank you Catherine Ferguson, friend who arrived in a perfect moment, and read each page with a true artist's eye.

Also, I thank everyone who has fed and clothed me the last couple of years.

Introduction

God has the strangeness of undiscovered islands.
—Robert Sencourt

I live in the Land of Enchantment, where rumors are taken to heart. In June 1994, a rumor made its way to New Mexico that angels were appearing on the Los Angeles freeways. The highway patrol had pulled over cars that began to slightly swerve. One patrolman listened as a woman tried to explained how she had become distracted when an angel appeared in her car. She said, "Officer, you may think I'm crazy, but an angel just announced that the first trumpet is about to sound." The officer shook his head, "No, you're the fourth person who has told me that story today."

In that same year, my husband had a dream wherein the morning star, Venus, was moving on the horizon. The word Venus (from the Latin venio) signifies to rush, to fall, to happen—words descriptive of the accelerations of modern times. In the dream, the entire sky was altering and glaciers in peach-light were calving in the distance.

Another dimension was breaking through. The world had become so flooded and dark; now all people on Earth were waiting for something. Then all heard a great shout in their mind and were relieved upon seeing the return of the morning star.

When Venus returns full circle as the morning star, the Stella Matutina (Latin), the Creator centers the world again.

Carl Jung, the Swiss psychiatrist, viewed the strange skies after World War II—the "flying saucers"—as portents of a massive alteration in the psyche of modern humanity. He intuited that UFO's are a symbol of the soul that is now alien intelligence. When this psychic split is healed, said Jung, humanity will become whole. UFO, modern mandala. More recently, in fields of wheat and barley are crop circle glyphs, messages left by a non-human intelligence. The skies are altering and the earth is in transition. New cosmic energies are showering the earth. The children of the Blue Ray are then born en masse after the turn of this century—though I have seen a few of you around in the Land of Enchantment.

Many are born with the inner eye open, and rediscover ancient sites, big dreams. They encounter the meaning of the artificial D&M Pyramid and the Face on Mars. History will be retold in its truth. The shamans will be recast and every culture will have its version.

Everything is changing.

As wisdom increases, false governments naturally fall away. The individual walks with Lady Liberty again. Art flourishes. The tools of evening are put back into the hands of the Creator. Free energies are released to the world by independent scientists. The World Wide Web becomes less a snare, and more a mycelia of organic networks that bring true imagination. A healing fire is discovered and spreads over the globe.

I hope we are ready.

THE CROSSING

A park doe crosses
the road for blossoms.
She is in my headlights,
does not know where to leap.
Her eyes are big, but she
does not know where to leap.

Chapter 1

Beauty and Love:
Transcendental and Immanent Objects

"We might equally call the unfathomable depth in the image, love, or at least say we cannot get to the soul of the image without love for the image."

—James Hillman, from *A Blue Fire*

$\mathcal{I}$ had a dream of a blue flower—more vivid than any I have seen in physical life. Its color and vibrations were magical fluctuations, mysteriously both mortal and immortal. This inner flower—a lyrical and fluidal unity between self, nature, and beyond—has since become for me the soul of all outer flowers.

Socrates was said to have been able to stare at the moon, immobile for hours, while in deep contemplation. This was not considered normal behavior by his peers, but they sensed his greatness and did not interfere. To Socrates, the moon was a dim representation of another celestial sphere seen mostly in the mind. Socrates saw in the moon an object of light, beauty, and perfect motion. He knew his mind moved like the moon.

In his memoirs, *The Memories*, Carl Jung wrote of a girl who dreamt she was on the moon.[1] When a female colleague, Dr. Marie-Louise von Franz, suggested to Jung that the girl had been "just dreaming she was on the moon," Jung replied that she had been on the real moon. She then realized that Jung meant that the moon of the psyche was the real moon, and that the physical moon in the sky is an illusion. This insight would take her "ten years to digest."[2]

The psyche is millions of years old. Its meaning is "soul"—the deepest source of life within human beings. It is also the immortal spirit pervading all of nature and each human being. Beauty and psyche were here on earth long before Homo sapiens arrived. In his book, *Coming Back*, Raymond Moody recounts a past-life regression when he was a "proto-human," a prehistoric version of man: "Although I was this ape-like creature, I had an appreciation of beauty. I know this because we chose a pretty place to live."[3] At our dawning, a transcendental object, beauty, was already there. The early humans finding a place to live had an image already within them to anticipate, at least subconsciously, what such a place would be. We have glimpses, a longing, for what lies mostly dormant in us. That longing is for more than food or clothes. There is a spiritual impulse to it. The nature of psyche is both inherent in us, and somehow independent of us. Psyche is an evolutionary beckoning that says "Oh yes, come this way." There are immanent divine impulses in nature. In the dark leafy forests beyond the glare stir magical deer, or nixies, wood-nymphs. A child thief holding something wild. Such beings have been around a long time. In the age when human consciousness was first awakening, such beings would even sit near one on a log. Adorable, but cause for a bit of dread. A man or woman entangled with such a magical being might fall into such entrancement that they would never emerge again. A lure to the numinous, a compelling to something more. A man or woman may then suffer what is called a "divine discontent." Meanwhile, the wood-nymph has escaped back to the depths, untouched, magical, timeless.

There is a true story about a man and his succubus. A succubus is a female spirit, often considered evil, that visits a person at night in their dreams. The story concerns a man who lived in the 1400s and had been in prison for forty years. During that time he had fallen in love with a succubus. When the man was finally offered freedom, he refused. He would not leave his cell, for his succubus was there, and he was in love with her. More strange is the story of a man in 1468 who was condemned to death for running a brothel filled with succubi.

The poet Rilke wrote: "The first part of beauty is terror." On display at Florence's Archaeological Museum are two bronze statues, bearded warriors, created during Greece's Golden Age. Both statues were retrieved from the Mediterranean Sea in 1972 in shallow water off Riace, Italy. Presumably, the Carthaginians pilfered them, then lost the statues at sea. Each bronze warrior weighs about a thousand pounds and is seven feet tall. A reporter wrote of the statues as: "presences of extraordinary power—so much that they command, and even tyrannize, the visitor's attention. The crowds move as if magnetized by a supernatural force. Cries of admiration are continually heard, but they are mixed with expressions of awe and even of terror." [4]

In the Greek story of Pygmalion, a young sculptor of Cyprus felt he could keep his soul in stone. He would sculpt what he thought a perfect woman looked like. Because he loathed real life women, he began immediate work on a statue of a maiden. Then, of course, he fell in love with it, so gorgeous it was, and perfectly represented his unconscious need. Then he kissed her. He took her in his arms. He brought gifts to her—flowers, birds. She remained stone. He dreamt she accepted his gifts. He awoke; she did not. He became very unhappy; he was suffering with what is called a "loss of soul." But then the goddess Venus knew what he wanted. And the statue became the living woman, Galatea.

One is not always given a flesh and blood rendition of their soul. In 1962, a Malaysian tribal man wished to marry a young woman who repeatedly spurned him and then married another. The man said that the woman had given him a melody in his dreams, and although another man had her body, he had her "dream soul." [5]

The melody the Malaysian man heard is a kind of kin to the idea of courtly love. In the eleventh to thirteenth centuries were the troubadours, those poets from the land called Langue d 'Oc—or The Language of the Yes (which was not the name of a territory, but of a common language covering parts of France and Spain). The troubadours introduced courtly, romantic love, wherein the soul's counterpart is seen in another person. This love transcended the traditions of society and its arranged marriages. It was an experience of the individual, and thus it was considered once to be adultery, punishable by death. But to the troubadours, the worst punishment was the loss of the beloved; it was better to have loved and face eternal Hell than to be without the beloved. This love was a transcendent object separate from the Church, State, and worldly ideas of Heaven and Hell. It is the troubadours who introduced romantic love to Christianity. I wrote such a love poem to my husband, Marc:

THE LAST WHITE LOCK

I still cling
to shy roses
and talk of rainstorms
instead of the eyes
I am climbing into
asking you what is bluer
the dream or the slender stem
the crush of blue

I have grace
I walk the beautiful spiral
staircase to you
I open the last white lock
of the heart

Do not wait
to turn to me
I give you roses
the way dreams send angels
I give you the whole mystery
the sun the smell of roses
burnt in air

With the eyes of love we can find the image of the eternal soul. For the romantic, this love is often an elusive and unrequited one. An image in the mind that reality cannot tarnish. A pursuing, but never having, a sweet sadness like a melancholy. The romantic would not have it any other way.

EVERY ANGEL IS NOT STEADFAST

I waited a long time for you
that day on the water

in reverie
I looked into it
but found only me

the bark peeled away from my heart

I have not
convinced you
of the water
of my feeling

the etched beauty on it
the lonely scribble up the stem

Unrequited love has sweetness, but betrayal in love is the cruelest lesson. In the 1949 film *The Heiress*, a wealthy but shy and unsophisticated spinster, Catherine, falls in love with a scammer, Morris, who pretends to fall in love, pursuant only of her money. Enamored, Catherine waits one night for Morris at the top of the stair. She waits but he doesn't arrive. She resigns to her room in bitter grief. Years later, there is a knock. Morris begs to be let in. She does not answer. Catherine's aunt asks why she is "cruel," for "Morris is a feather in any woman's hat." Catherine answers that she learned cruelty from masters, meaning Morris and her father. Morris betrayed her love for money, and her father's Victorian values on how an upper-class woman should impress herself on society is his betrayal. But as Morris hammers on the door, there is great pain pressed into her heart.

What has more power than Love? In ancient Greece, love as Eros is well described by Diogenes, who wrote of an athlete: "I have seen the victor Dioxippos subdue all contenders at Olympia and be thrown on his back by the glance of a girl."[6] In modern America, driving along a highway, I heard over the radio the same force of Eros in a female singer who sang the lyrics, "If love were a train I'd throw my body right down on the track."

Love always suggests finding beauty in a thing. This "seeing" that is "in the eye of the beholder" pours itself on beings not always so apparent in their beauty. This higher love graces us all. In fact, there is a divine objective love wherein each thing is in the eye of God. But subjective love is where we start, and it too is authentic. In Hollywood, the theme of a personal love is enacted by stars greater than life as a way to convey what modern troubadours see in their loves. This is good for the mind's eye and the heart's imagination. However, a Venus or an Adonis is sometimes best seen on screen, because such a character may not be accessible at the personal level. Nunnally Johnson once said of Marilyn Monroe in an interview in 1960, "She is a phenomenon of nature, like Niagara Falls or the Grand Canyon. You can't talk to it. It can't talk to you. All you can do is sit back and be in awe of it."

A love then lands more real than angelfood. Come stars, come starfish, and oceanic matter manifestations. For this precedes history. Even the insect wants sun—transcendence. But I am content in this moment with this physical manifestation. I think this is everything, yet anything physical eventually appears accidental. The amber sap in weeping trees stopped in time. The quickening of the old blood, maple wood-warmed in sun.

A TENT FOR THE SUN

I wish to enjoy myself
simply in this sun.

You have gone down to the sand
to wash, your hair fluttering
like a starfish

I have found you
and press a star
into the mud, one part of mind
in love with another

I want only
to enjoy this moment

I think, this is everything,
our minds are an endless advance,
a prehistoric fly caught in amber
still waits for another flight

are you deception?
never answer the question

this is everything
the sun, insects
the swiftness of my pulse

Chapter 2

The Divine Feminine

"They say I came for all, but in truth I came for her Who came for all. For it had come to pass that there were those who had lost their way and, lacking in spark, could not return into the fullness; seeing this, She came unto them, giving Her life to the depths of matter."

–The Logos, from the Ecclesia Gnostica Mysteriorum.[1]

"She wears an Egyptian ring that sparkles before she speaks."

–Bob Dylan

I had a dream wherein I viewed a blue planet below in space. I knew it was Earth because it was so beautiful. I was then given a book that was called The Bachelor Planet. I read that a wedding was about to take place. I wondered, who is the bride? When I awoke, I thought about a man well-known in Santa Fe who walks about in a long white satin dress. His beard is like that of Walt Whitman's; his poetry akin to Blake's. He claims that he is married to the earth. It has been said that when a woman puts on men's clothes she is merely stealing social power, but when a man puts on women's clothes he is searching for God. It is ironic that we have been lost and are seeking Her, for She is right here, a less abstract being than the Logos. She is this particular space and time, and this particular body. All the creatures of nature are spun from Her, the mysterious leaven within, the sensual food that celebrates life as it is here.

In Proverbs, Wisdom invites, "Come, eat of my bread, and drink of the wine which I have mingled," which is what one did for wedding feasts in the Old Testament. She is also "a tree of life to those who lay hold of her: and happy is everyone that retaineth her." She is a generous, life-affirming being. She is waiting in the wings.

Yet, Wisdom "sought a dwelling place among humanity, but found none." Therefore She has withdrawn again and "has taken her seat among the angels" (1 Enoch 42:1-2). Wisdom reminds us, "When there were no depths, I was brought forth; when there were no fountains abounding with water . . . When he prepared the heavens, I was there; when he set a compass upon the face of the depth." (Proverbs 8:27).

Robert Bly, author and poet, calls Her "The Mysterious Hidden Woman," and believes Her resurgence was the major cultural event of the late fifties and early sixties when She took the form of Cybele, the Roman goddess of chaos, drums, flutes, ingenious dress and dance; the natural body, the psychedelic mind, music and poetry.[2] The god of wine, Dionysus was there also. The dove, a transcendent addition related more to Sophia, was symbol for peace and the politics of hope. People slept in the park, in a new Eden. One young man learned to grow sweet potatoes, and could play the sweet potato musically. Innocence. But we fell on them "like a stone" and She was oppressed again. The poet Etheridge Knight wrote the following "Hard Rock" poem:

> she opened
> to me like a flower
> but I fell on her
> like a stone
> I fell on her like a stone

There are two aspects of the Goddess. The first and oldest is known as the Great Mother, her names Cybele, Kali, Spider Woman, the Black Goddess. She is the universe materia itself. She is thus the womb that births us cyclically into nature. We eventually return to that womb. We are of the prima materia that passes away,

9

as all physical universes eventually pass away. The Black Goddess may be, in modern physics terms, the dark matter of the universe. This ninety-five to ninety-nine percent of the unseen universe of which we know almost nothing, is necessary for the structure of the universe and the fate of all created matter. The other aspect is the Goddess as transcendental being, the fruition of the feminine body as matter. She births a mirrory star on water, a conscious spark in matter that can reach the universal archetypes of Sophia, Isis, and the Virgin Mary. Born also of the womb, but then able to reach full archetypal consciousness that is immortal, she sits on the throne in heaven, but she has never left nature:

> Tell me everything,
> New bees start up in this mad clover
> our nets lift, fall
> at the avenues
> A knowing beneath our feet,
> a quiet seeding of ferns,
> a falling into inner woman
> we wait on some edge, to breathe

Earth and the Great Mother abounded in fertility and agricultural societies in ancient times. In Greece, the Eleusinian Mysteries were dedicated to Demeter, Hades, Persephone. In Athens, initiates would first bathe in the sea, then march to Eleusis in procession. Ceremonies followed in the evening with fasting and the sharing of sacred drink. Through ecstasy one could enter the soul of nature both psychologically and at a biologically enhanced level. Goddess is ecstasy (or an "ec" meaning "out" of stasis. In the Greek, ecstasy means "the withdrawal of the soul from the body"). Such a state of bliss is relevant to entering the greater body of Mother Nature, and even into the experience that near-death encounters bring.

The Romans called her Cybele; on her crown is depicted a miniature city wall. Her priests worshiped her with cries and shouts, cymbals and drums. Worship was orgiastic. Mythical attendants were wild, half-demonic beings, priests dressed in drag. Frenzied music and dancing sometimes culminated in self-mutilation and sheer exhaustion. Then, some time in history, things went to emotional debacle, to orgies and sensationalized spirituality. Terence McKenna theorizes that the culprit was when these earth societies switched from mushroom cults to beer cults. The depiction of the "hairy-footed Bacchus" shows up then, writes Terence—which is associated with antisocial behaviors and profanities that excessive alcohol consumption brings.[3]

The church fathers were appalled, and they have been put off by the whole thing ever since. To the patriarchy, disorder is the antithesis of the sacred. Apollo versus Dionysus. The Apollonian mind is more distanced from nature, whereas the Dionysian and Cybele intoxications can flood the individual back into the oceanic primal unity—a biological and transbiological consciousness. The god Apollo stands above, in an air almost too thin for humans, having his own exquisite beauty. This is perfection. The price may be that one becomes static, secure, constipated, and dead of soul. In a drive-in church in Miami, Florida, one can listen to a full sermon through a speaker attached to the car. One need never leave the car, never talk to anyone, nor touch the ground. But in modern dreams, the Great Mother often appears as a mother bear, representing the dangerous split-off aspect of the prima materia, ready to devour.

Where is our mother? Researchers have traced the DNA found in mitochondria passed from mother to daughter back to southern Africa. Thus, all women share the same mother, as do all men, since man comes from a woman's womb. We may all share the same ancestral mother or Eve, back in Africa. Is it any wonder that Africa is a place where so many leave their heart?

THE MORTAL PART OF FEELING

Eve with apple
in her hand,
an erosion of light

we bear the longing
over having
the object of the shadow
we eat

we have no mother
we are haunted as a shoe in wheat

the sun, blue as ravens

the place of hunger
the loss of the mother

She is both earth and gardenlike heaven, the terra-cotta dove, in the art of 4500 B.C. Mesopotamia. Those that find her find the Tree of Life. Doves released onto humanity, restore humanity. She is there. A muse. A guide to the depth of things, both personal and transpersonal.

We find mysterious tracks . . .

DOVE IN THE FOREST

She is letting go
of doves that fall
from a luminous place

branches touch, motion
of light
the last edges of wind
inside her

hardwoods, slant of blue sun
she moves through cold air
making snowy tracks
falls into abstract radiance

in the white air
pages loosen
from her fingers

she leaves the impression
of a beautiful absence
silent woods, blue shadows
doves that hide in snow

She lives both in a heaven near us and in the earth at our feet. She is the leaven in the bread we eat, the ascension embodied in Isis and Sophia, stars. An inexplicable light, a sensual immersion. Youth at its most Edenic, she stays somewhere near her creatures, a presence never completely vanished. She is the magnetic force that draws us, and the child in us that picks the flowers and runs to her saying, "This is for you." Ultimately she is the chalice of the early Grail legends, a Celtic Christianity where nature and God had not yet parted.

IN HER GARDEN,
ENCROACHING ON THE IRIS
(for Princess Diana)

We hear a faint crunch
in the iris,
the light of a rabbit
spooks

She steps into the iris, the air
is gardeny
a crisp, white
hunger

the rabbit senses Her,
her form
taps the eye,
her voice shimmers
a soprano leaf

the rabbit
dare not move
for this is stunning

She breathes like a Venus sky,
her feet beautify
like a chalice

wherever she steps
the rabbit loves her,
she ripens the air
fruit ignites

"She is far away, but ever near, a frequent characteristic of Sophia . . . When we deal with Sophia, we will find ourselves alternately dazzled and blindfolded," writes author Caitlin Matthews.[4]

She is not confined to institutions; in fact, she appears outside them, for they are often blind to her. She was even witnessed by Muslims in Cairo, Egypt, seen with "doves of light moving at high speed about her."[5] She is appearing to many, so that we remember. I had a dream on remembering a song. God spoke from a beam of light with lightning in it. Behind me was an ocean and a microphone. A crowd gathered on the beach and people would march up one at a time to sing into the microphone. If they sang the right song, then doves circled in the air above. If it was the wrong song, a circle of ravens would appear instead. The ocean would muscle up behind, a thick blue wall. The crowd would say, "Try to remember."

To "re-member" is to bring the members back together. We remember Isis, whose husband Osiris dies, his dismembered pieces all over Egypt. She reassembles him, each piece "re-membered"— minus his phallus, which was swallowed by a fish. Isis has been equated with Demeter gathering grain (Osiris is the grain). The goddess Isis assembles her husband personally—a feminine power. But Ezekiel witnesses in the Valley of Bones, the masculine God resurrecting the bones of an army, fleshing them out from afar, en masse.

We sit on the lap of the Goddess for she is Earth, more personally accessible. The Egyptian Pharaoh sits on the throne of Isis, the goddess whose child is Horus. The Goddess later merges in the motif of the Madonna in whose lap is the savior Jesus, for Logos needs the lap, the foundation of Earth.

Notes:

—Mitochondria are thought to be descendants of Pre-Cambrian bacteria that "invaded" our cells in a symbiotic relationship. Thus, they were once an alien being to us. The tiny chromosomes of mitochondria can be traced back to an original host. It is quite likely that the original mother (Eve, or a small group of genetically linked mothers) lived in Africa. Eve was not the only female hominid

200,000 years ago. Homo erectus and Neanderthal were contemporaries. (Lloyd Pye, author of *Everything You Know is Wrong. Book One: Human Origins* by Adamu Press, 1997, U.S.A., is an excellent resource.)

The egg passes cytoplasm filled with mitochondria to the next generation; the sperm does not. Though intact overall, some of the mitochondrial genes have been lost, and some transferred out of the cytoplasm into the nucleus of the cell, into the chromosomes of the host.

—Dark matter may be the void, the zero-point vacuum energy, from which spins visible matter. Dark matter, or the void, is really light, photonic. Beyond or behind the veil of dark matter may be the First Mover, or First Cause.

Chapter 3

The Divine Masculine

"the God that answereth by fire, let him be God."

–I Kings 18:24

Over millennia there has been a dialogue between the heavens and human beings, between an abstract male God and his creatures. By way of the Logos, which draws mental images and ideas down to the material world, the divine masculine manifests. Logos has been called a "second God," and a "heavenly Adam" that mediates between Creator and humankind.[1] It enters the world from above as Light.

Prophets are "second gods," who bring the light and word of heaven to a generation. The prophet Elijah of the Old Testament not only speaks for his heavenly Lord, he does healings on the sick, and raises a boy from the dead. Sure of his Lord's supremacy, he makes a bet with the worshipers of the god Baal, saying, "the God that answereth by fire, let him be God." But when Baal is called upon to be a fire and consume a bull sacrifice, there is "no voice." Elijah then prepares his own bull, pouring water on it for extra effect. He calls on the Lord, and the "fire of the Lord" falls, and consumes the bull. Winning the bet, Elijah commands that all the priests of Baal be slain. Then he departs into the wilderness wishing for death, guilt ridden for his deed. Then, the Lord passes by in a great wind that breaks rocks to pieces. And though "the word of the Lord came to him," the "Lord is not seen in the wind." A voice then tells him to anoint Elisha "to be prophet." The story ends with Elijah, who casts his mantle to Elisha, like one saying to another, "Now, you be the prophet."

Yahweh, Lord of the Old Testament, is very alien. His name is never to be pronounced; the vowels remain up in the mind. The strange energies are caught up in the sky, taking Elijah to heaven in a whirlwind chariot of fire. The energies are also in Moses coming down from Mount Sinai after an encounter with God, when the "skin of his face shone" (Exodus 34:30), the rays of light are brought down to humankind.

The Logos appears to come from another dimension because our minds are still building a bridge to it. When God appeared through Logos to Moses in the burning bush, Moses hid his face, for this was God. Logos can pipeline through natural processes. Reductionists, however, have suggested that Moses was either "hallucinating" or else saw only the brilliant blossoms of one of the Mimosa families, the desert acacia. It insults the intelligence of desert peoples to suggest that they could not differentiate between local flora and an experience like "the burning bush." Bushes also relate to eyelashes in ancient Egypt, and when they "burn" this means that the third eye is open. The term "hallucination" is commonly bandied about when no one has a clue about a phenomenon. The fiery bush may have been the light brain talking—the new brain breaking into the ordinary human mind, which steps aside and allows another kind of mind to enter. One sees with heavenly eyes and ears. One sees the forms of the Logos. Homer was blind, yet the Iliad is a drama with zoom-lens like photos of "shining" helmets, and the "clanging" spears of warriors. One may "see" and "hear" after a period of extreme stress, or after a mystical experience when a person has been psychologically "broken." The Light can then come through, be it the Christ-light or Bliss or Nirvana. Michelangelo was assigned the almost impossible task of painting the Sistine Chapel. He nearly gave up and destroyed his creation until one day he "saw" in his mind and in clouds, the entire ceiling painted, finished. Van Gogh saw a Logos so animated and brilliant that his contemporaries hid their faces from his flowers, his gorgeously raging yellows.

The source of creativity from the Solar Logos is at first "beheld" in the mind. It is from inner senses first that one sees and hears, which later flesh out in earthly, physical forms. In the Book of Genesis, the Logos creates forms in some image of God. It is God's mind made flesh. God says, "Let there be" and then the image comes whole—the entire earth, the waters, dry land, herbs and fruit, etc. Genesis is at least partly about God's psyche, written in stunning poetry which is revelation more beautiful than a fact sheet, and is psychically more accurate. Logos is based on a perception of wholes. It is like intuitive art in which whole pictures appear in the mind first, and then are expressed after. Pablo Picasso, the cubist artist with a personality as forceful as the Old Testament God, announced to the world, "I don't develop, I am!"[2] For Logos, imagery and sound is not thinking per se, nor the kind of mind or reason interested in solving mazes and crossword puzzles. It is certainly more than a computer program no matter how sped up the program. Never mistake a computer language which is one directional, with a brilliant dialogue with Logos. Logos is a part of the fundamental structure of ordering of the universe and is the link to higher dimensional worlds. In the Book of Genesis, the Hebraic letters project shadow shapes that are of a tetrahedral geometry of hyperdimensionality. This tetrahedral geometry is also found in sacred monuments around the world, in the Sphinx and Great Pyramid at Giza, Stonehenge, as well as in the crop circles.[3] Mathematician Stan Tenen took a spiral of a tube torus and put it inside a three-dimensional tetrahedron and shined light through it. By doing so, he was able to generate all the letters of the Hebrew, Greek, and Aramaic alphabets.[4] (A tube torus is snake-like in form; a tetrahedron is a pyramid.) Emanuel Swedenborg wrote that a little paper was sent to him from heaven on which a few words were written in Hebrew letters. It said that every letter involved an arcana of wisdom that was in the inflections and curvatures of the letters, and also in the sounds.[5] In Matthew 5:18 it is written: "Till heaven and earth pass away, one iota or one little horn [i.e., of a letter] shall not pass from the law."

In Eden, the Lord walks as knowledge-made-flesh, a physical God, even if still somewhat abstracted, almost a visitor. There is a forbidden fruit. An untouchable thing—a fruit beyond human senses. The command not to eat the one fruit is a first Law and a change in perception—an act which separates God from his creatures. When Eve did take the fruit to be more like God, (a symbolic fruit, for there were no apples in the Holy Land; there was a plethora of apricots) she and Adam became self-conscious beings; the light brain began to shine.

There is another form of Logos—very old, a more connective, organic light, more feminine in nature. It landed millennia ago, its mycelium gracing the planet. Symbiotic and enhancing, the hallucinogenic mushrooms have been credited by the botanist and shamanistic explorer Terence McKenna for humanity's ability to commune with each other at the level of human self-reflection, meaningful language, and visionary experience. Shamans have used the "talking mushrooms" for centuries upon centuries, calling some of them, "flesh of the gods." Terence McKenna states that the psilocybin mushrooms, when ingested, complete the human nervous system via interaction with the neurotransmitters of our brain chemistry, and are thus a key to the growth spurt in our brain's evolution. Terence writes that the mushroom, Stropharia cubensis, for example, is "Older than human thought and older than the human species."[8] Its mycelia networks can cover acres and may have more connections than the neurons in the human brain.[7] These mycelial networks are in "hyperlight communication across space and time."[8] Mushroom spores can survive outer space, have casings that approach that of metals, and they are deep purple which absorbs the ultraviolet end of the light spectrum. Nearly immortal, mushrooms may have much to tell when ingested, like the "rolls" given prophets in the Old Testament.

A "hyperlight communication across space and time" is now speaking to us upon the earth in the form of crop circles. Crop circles are those mysterious interweavings of bent stalks—not broken—but swirled and flattened patterns in fields of wheat and other cereal crops, creating pictograms with spurs, combs, dumbbells, and circles with rings and bars. Witnesses have seen lights, even a "golden star" over fields prior to a formation. A buzzing sound like loud crickets, or an unusual wind passing, has been reported (like Elijah's wind?). A feeling of deep connection is also experienced by many people. When entering a circle, its border, one may sense the invitation to the future, which is inscribed in our human subconscious deciphering a new language.

The Celtic cross, as well as Vedic and Hopi symbols, are manifesting, though no circles have been fully decoded. Some circles have been interpreted as warnings about the earth's environment, and humankind's state. Mother Earth is sacred. Logos warns the money changers from the temple. The crop circles are concentrated in Great Britain, and most are in the relative vicinity of Stonehenge, Silbury, and Avebury, but they have been found all over the world, and date back at least to the Middle Ages. They have a tendency toward ancient sites, and especially Celtic sites, whose history of a Christianity not severed from paganism may be a salient point. The Celtic cross has been identified in some of them, and also designs that denote the breaking apart of the cosmic egg, producing a sacred child.

Crop circles have increased in number and complexity since 1990 and 1991, each circle building on the pattern before, leading some researchers to say that a dialogue is taking place with humankind. One may wonder what the final manifestation will be. British researcher Colin Andrews states, "The Final Manifestation will be of a physical kind to unite humankind to be in its natural order." This hyperlight is Logos writing on the earth like a tablet, an anvil that strikes gently and democratically for all to see, though we may still need a modern Moses to decode its messages. In his book, *The Gift*, Doug Ruby, a commercial airline pilot, has discerned that the crop circle patterns are a model for a "ship" and also a power plant that creates free, non-polluting energy from the earth's ley lines. The physics and shape of the ship and power plant are seen when the crop circle pictogram is raised in three dimensions and then spun. When spinning, wheels within wheels, and fields of energy within fields arise in an eerie blur that is electromagnetic in nature. In high rotation, the physics of the ship run in coherence, or in harmonic frequencies, dialogues with the zero-point energy which is the vacuum from wherein we all arise (the First Mover or First Cause in this universe). The message is heard in its spin—as a recording tape or music album must rotate in order to manifest its being. (Ezekiel 1:16 describes the ship with "a wheel in the middle of a wheel.")

Johann Blomeyer, a diviner acknowledged by the Dalai Lama, says the circles are two dimensional fingerprints of an incoming beam of consciousness.[9] This incoming consciousness affects people not only at the actual point of contact with the earth but for hundreds of miles around. Johann has divined this energy as being directed through the Solar Logos. It is a double cone or diamond shaped beam of consciousness, ultrasonic in nature above ground and infrasonic below, with electromagnetic properties. The energy travels to the core of the planet. Each crop circle is a two-dimensional cross-sectional representation of the incoming beam. In 1988, a motorist in the vicinity saw a constant beam of white light which stretched from the clouds to the ground near Silbury Hill.[10]

In the Old Testament we see cloudy pillars that stand in the desert, and at the Tabernacle which is the Lord's. A cloud, but not the face of the heavenly God. Are we ever to see the face of the Logos? Or will we be like Moses, half shielded, when that Old Testament God said, "Thou canst not see my face. I will put thee in a clift of the rock, and will cover thee with my hand while I pass by: And I will take away mine hand, and thou shalt see my back parts: but my face shall not be seen." (Exodus 33:20-23).

ABSTRACT GRASS

The moon over the plain
is forever in freefall

abstract grass turns leaf
into calf into soul

Soon it is standing, runs
clothed with the senses
turns and nibbles
the grass

An angel begins his own
slow course of descent
into World

but Earth is not his home

the timothy stalls him a little

Notes:

—The plants in crop circles show molecular changes suggestive of microwave energy, but the changes have not been duplicated in any lab. The changes also relate to ultrasound effects.

—The pillar-clouds in the Old Testament may well be God making strange alien visits. The God without a face comes and goes, is capricious, as is the vacuum zero-point energy which also "travels" in clouds despite being everywhere. Both the Old Testament God and the vacuum energy are a strange intelligence to us, omnipresent, and yet not always available. That is, present free-energy machines and levitrons mysteriously have periods of perfect operability mixed with interludes when they don't operate (are dependent on clouds of the vacuum energy drifting by).

—What could be more "other" than the God of the Old Testament? Perhaps human, or alien technology. Read *The Spaceships of Ezekiel* by Josef F. Blumrich (Bantam Books, 1974. NY, NY). Blumrich was the designer of the Saturn V rocket, as well as Chief of Systems Layout for NASA in the 1960s. This background gave him a unique ability to see clearly what the visions of Ezekiel were really trying to describe, which he maintains was an air-to-surface landing craft, whose technology was not that much further advanced over what we have today.

—The old brain, the cerebellum, is associated with telepathy and fire-walking. See the work of Joseph Chilton Pearce, especially his book, *Magical Child*.

Chapter 4

The Blue Ray

"She breathes like a Venus sky,

her feet beautify like a chalice."

—Angela Menking

*T*he skies seem to be "quickening," a term used by radio host and author Art Bell. His book, *The Quickening*, is a record of the cascade of discoveries and novelties taking place on Earth and in the heavens: mutations, weather changes, space shuttles and the ozone hole, technology, genetics, astral and planetary events. The whole world is beginning to watch the skies and the mind of humanity, as if moving from station to station to some finale wherein an entire paradigm shift occurs.

Many cultures view this time as the end of a cycle. The Vatican has its observatory at Graham Mountain in Arizona. The Hopi Indians of the southwestern United States prophesied a new blue star appearing at the beginning of a new world. The "Blue Star" did appear on February 23, 1987 when it erupted in the Greater Magellanic Cloud of the Milky Way. A giant supernova (SN 1987A), it flashed intense radiation directly to Earth equal in amount to all the stars and galaxies in the visible universe. The neutrinos (chargeless, massless particles) that preceded the shock wave raced through the Earth's south pole. The supernova occurred at seven plus degrees of Aquarius. The symbol of seven degrees is, an astrologer said, "A Child is Seen Being Born out of an Egg." Cosmic ray particles can produce mutations, and a new root race/age of humanity. Supernova 1987A "will shine again in the southern skies around 2005" reported USA Today on June 10, 1997 (due to the debris of the original explosion smashing back into the star). The Hopi say the Blue Star heralds the Great Purification.

In July 1994, Jupiter was being impacted by a comet with effects perhaps more profound than at first glance. Comets may eject genetic material into planetary space. In the case of Jupiter, its space and nature are very sun-like. Its atmosphere is like our Sun's, being comprised of eighty-four to eighty-eight percent hydrogen and eleven percent helium. Jupiter contains seventy percent of all the mass in the solar planets—is greater than 318 Earths in mass—but is only twenty-five percent the density of Earth due to its gaseous constituents. Jupiter emits to Earth more energy than it receives from the Sun. Jupiter is at least 1400 Earths in volume, and numerous moons (sixteen known satellites) orbit it like planets around a sun. In July 1994, fragments of a comet called Shoemaker Levy 9, traveling sixty times faster than a bullet, hit Jupiter with the kinetic energy of six million megatons of TNT. If Jupiter had been hit with enough force (even artificially, as with a plutonium load), it might have become a white dwarf, and we on earth would see two suns, the second sun being Jupiter, which would appear to be about the size of the moon to the natural eye. As an emitting sun, what might its rays doused with comet dust bring?

A binary star system for Earth has been envisioned by different seers. Jupiter is a rather dramatic candidate for becoming the second sun. Another conjecture is that the star system Sirius A and B will move closer to Earth in a new alignment and create a binary system for Earth.

Gordon Michael Scallion states that a new sun will appear blue in the evening sky and the light cast will cause a blue tint to the skin of all races. He foresees children of a new root race being born after the turn of this century. (Scallion accurately predicted Hurricane Andrew, the Mississippi River floods, and many modern earthquakes).

This new root race of humankind may be partly due to cosmic events. Jupiter, as a sun, would be able to emit rays and energies from a hyperdimensional realm, since stars may be viewed as portals having a metaphysics beyond being mere hydrogen furnaces (explained in Mars chapter). Suns as portals are metaphoric of birth canals wherein matter and light and celestial bodies spew. And it is more than metaphoric that the comet Shoemaker-Levy gravitated toward Jupiter's red eye. This eye is no simple storm—but an upwelling of hyperphysics.

In his book, *Beyond the Brain: Birth, Death and Transcendence*, by Dr. Stanislov Grof, a subject who was rebirthing on LSD, painted a fetus passing through a purifying fire into the celestial realm of a starry goddess.[1] On either side of the goddess was a painted peacock, each with its plumage of many eyes. I thought peacocks, eyes. Birds, comets. This painting by the rebirthing subject is reminiscent of one of the Isis myths, wherein Isis puts a king's child into a purifying fire, in order that its mortal body be burned away, that the child may be reborn into a more starry place. The goddess takes children even beyond the biological in order that they may ascend to heaven. She does not devour her children, though she may, as with the king's child, momentarily abduct. Later, she unites with Osiris and the child that is born from them is Horus (born of the genes of Isis, or a genesis). Her child, Horus, the All-Seeing Eye, is the God within All that sees.

In the Book of Revelation, a woman clothed with the Sun appears in the heavens, is with child, laboring in birth. As the child's time nears, there is "another wonder in heaven," the appearance of a great red dragon which stands before the woman, ready to devour the child. However, when the child is born, it is "caught up to God and his throne," and the woman, given two wings of a great eagle, flees into the wilderness, where she is nourished. Meanwhile, the deceiver, Satan, and his angels, cast out of heaven and "into the earth," make war on the remnant of her seed.

Earth is therefore blocked from heaven's child for awhile. The marriage of the Christ child, the Lamb, with the receptive church of humanity will wait until after the great purification. In Revelation, John writes of an angel standing in the sun that cried in a loud voice at Armegeddon, the final purification:

> saying to all the fowls that fly in the midst of heaven, Come and gather yourselves together unto the supper of the great God; that ye may eat the flesh of kings; the beast, and the kings of the earth, and their armies, gathered together to make war against him (Rev: 19:17).

In the book, *The Keys of Enoch*, by J. J. Hurtak, a new entity stands in the Sun.[2] The old entity/entities kept humanity from a dialogue with the Sun intelligence. Below is Key 117:

> The solar hierarchies and the princes of the earth have prevented man from being unified with the faithful of all universes. They have refused to accept karmic release and have dictated gospels of hatred and obliviousness so that man has not responded to the Shema—a radiant call to which unites us with YHWH in all universes. For this reason they are being removed from their regions of power.

A way for humanity, a dialogue, is beginning with celestial power. Though Earth is in a time of troubles now, humanity will transmute itself from a merely earth-bound creature to supernatural star-hood. We will change our nature from that of sheep to that of the divine Lamb.

In Revelation the antichrist and false prophet had "two horns like a lamb, and he spake as a dragon." Could the dragon be a symbol for DNA? The dragon cast into the earth where all his power is? For although the DNA code may be a key to physical and intellectual perfecting, the call of spirit is not to be locked out. When the spirit is part of this self-creation, full creature-hood may begin. Pray humanity does not clone its conscience after the Dark Ages, wherein a rooster was killed for laying eggs, being perceived as an abomination of nature. Also, as a nurse, I cannot imagine putting righteous platitudes before healing and easing of pain, and if genetics and cloning is in that compassionate spirit, then humanity has done a kindness.

But there is danger in trying to be a hero with this dragon. Dolly, the cloned sheep born near Edinburgh, Scotland in July 1996, came at the expense of many deformed and aborted lambs. Adamu, or Adam, Sumerian for "Primitive Worker," was created via genetic manipulation. The gods of Sumeria, the Annunkai, (as researched by Zecharia Sitchin in *Genesis Revisited*) selected either early hominids or more developed later humans, in the pursuit of an intelligent, if somewhat asleep, slave. Their manipulation of our genetics created many defects along the way, including difficult births through mutated pelvises.

The whole point is research and experiment, cross-special methods included. Firefly genes have been inserted into wheat, fish genes into corn, and I've heard a rumor of human nuclei into a swine ovum. Most experiments fail, as most natural mutations are not viable. Seeking health and harmony in nature may be tricky, as death and life, eating and being eaten are part of the balance. When the lamb and lion lie down together it may well not be due to the human genome project. Ironically, at the level of transplanting proteins from one species to another, the mammary glands of ewes and sows have been found to be best for foreign genes to activate, as in that tissue there is a natural ability to produce and export protein without harming the protein or the host. The mother's breast is receptive.

Surrogate mothers are fine for sheep. Dolly seems happy. Under whose jurisdiction will clones fall? Will they live on a farm? Will they fall before a God-like master to slave and sacrifice to another's whims? Will clones colonize Mars? Fuel the Department of Energy? Certainly they will have differing psyches, even some identical twin studies show great diversity at the level of psyche—one twin schizo-phrenic and one not, for example. For a great psyche and intelligence beyond the dragon throws out images and dreams that are not all nature and nurture. But transplanting genes for physical effects and dispositions may even cross the border into soul. Transplanting organs from one human to another is mysterious business. One woman received a heart-lung transplant from a teenage boy and dreamed of his name one night. (Names of organ donors are confidential. She also had his teenage cravings).

But the skies are quickening as much as the pace of any labs, and a change in our nature is at hand.

In 1917, three sheep-herding children in a hollow pasture called Cova da Iria, near the cave of St. Irene, in Fatima, Portugal, met with "Our Lady of Heaven" at scheduled intervals wherein they witnessed another sun. This sun would spin through the clouds, advancing down the valley to a tree. Shiny white petals fell out of the sky, but vanished when the children reached out to catch them, leaving a flash of light and a sweet fragrance. Then, the sun vanished up into the physical sun in the sky.

The Fatima sun, the spinning disc and rays, has been thought to symbolize the new energies that will be showering the earth. The psychic, Ray Stanford, who works in the tradition of Edgar Cayce, first experienced the Virgin Mary in the 1960s, and began to channel Fatima messages otherwise kept from the public by the Vatican. He predicts many changes, "some very frightening," both in the heavens and on the physical earth, will precede a new race of humankind. Stanford's prophecy warns that the Sun will be darkened for three days, and that people must stay in their homes. Many will die. Some will die of a "signal through the autonomic system that will literally kill the body physical."[3] Stanford writes that a "new root race" of humankind will be born at the end of this millennium, "some will be changed forever as bodies, even the genetic" and "a new tendency for a different coloration of eye," and "strange will be their eyes."[4]

The change in eye pattern is a striking detail. Iridology—the study of the iris of the eye, goes back as far as ancient Egypt. The iris is a map, holographic, of the entire body and brain. It is the only part of the brain tissue we see. The optic nerve is made up of millions of bundles of nerves and these nerves attach to the iris which mirrors all parts of the body. The iris records all bodily and emotional events, except those that occur while under anesthesia. Relevant to the Fatima prophecy is that if one generation heals itself, even of a genetic tendency, the next generation will have an iris free of the genetic weakness. Although iris patterns are far more important than color, those of African descent have had their eye color change from brown to blue. There is striking beauty in black skin and blue eyes. In 1975, at a hospital in Boca Raton, Florida, a black man was admitted who went into an epileptic seizure. My husband saw his eyes change from brown to blue. The man, in a severe healing crisis, experienced a dramatic change in the iris of his eyes.

It is not hard to imagine that whole generations will have a different coloration and pattern of eye if the whole earth goes through a major healing crisis. The Blue Ray incarnations come en masse in the future with a change in eye color and configuration. Even infants notice eyes. In fact, an infant focuses not only on a primary caregiver's face but intently on his/her eyes, mirroring and reaching for that image.

The patterns of the iris have been divided into three types:

1. Flowers—in youth they weren't nourished; they dance and sing to fill the cups. They have somewhat fragile constitutions.

2. Streams—psychic abilities; they easily pick up other's energies.

3. Jewels—in their head, intellectual, precise, they forget to feed themselves.

The above types may be found mixed in a person. What will be the eye characteristics of the children of the Blue Ray? In the book *Mass Dreams of the Future*, a group of subjects were hypnotically progressed into the future to the year 2050, and they reported that the eye color of humanity had changed, that the iris was a "deep violet."[5] (In the twentieth century, actress Elizabeth Taylor has nearly violet eyes, which is quite rare, but found in those with phenomenal constitutions.)

The human race, writes Stanford, may anticipate that at the end of the century "shall He (Jesus) appear, as one not born, yet in flesh, to walk and dwell among men." Many not seen on the earth in two thousand years shall also reincarnate, some through the "channels of birth and some not," meaning some return to Earth not through woman. Then shall there be "peace and a restoration of Godliness."[6]

The Goddess comes to us through the back door, and in simplicity. In a painting of the Virgin of Monserrat, the virgin is soon to give birth, discovered by shepherds in a cave in the hills. She wears simple wool. Wearing wool is a mystical Sufi way to the divine. The word Sufi is derived from the Arabic word for wool,

Suf, or the Persian word for pure, Saf. The word Sufi denotes wearing wool, and is derived from the word Sophia, meaning wisdom. The poet Rumi says, "Woman is a ray of God, She is not just the earthly beloved, she is creative, not created." Mary, the mother of Jesus, is very much revered by some Sufis, and she receives divinity in her womb.

SHEEP-WOMAN

She wears a blue
sheepskin coat, pockets soft
as nubile wombs

dreams float up,
more than sheep,
more than woman

she comes for strays
strewn like clothes
over the hills

lamb crouched in grass,
lamb with flower
in its mouth,
lamb with a blue cry

Come home, little sheep,
what ewe found you, what
angel herded you back
with the rest of the catch
smoky eyes in the flounder net

Do not be afraid, we worship
the little lamb we lure
We are like angels
fishing in the sheep wind.

Notes:

—In cloning, the entire nucleus, with its DNA, is inserted into another animal's ovum with cytoplasm, which contains mitochondrial DNA. In humans, mitochondrial DNA traces mother-daughter lineage back to one Eve, or to a genetically close-knit group of Eves. If human DNA is ever inserted into an animal ovum, then the mitochondrial DNA is lost.

Chapter 5

A Recipe From Lourdes

". . . out of his belly shall flow rivers."

–John (7:37)

$\mathcal{I}$ n February 1858, a peasant girl from the village of Lourdes in Southern France had a vision. She was told by a lady apparition to dig in the muddy earth, which uncovered a spring. From this spring still flows 27,000 gallons of water a day. The water apparently heals four million pilgrims every year. The Medical Bureau at Lourdes has substantiated sixty-five cures since 1858—including tuberculosis and blindness. The spring at Lourdes has high amounts of ozone. Ozone and hydrogen peroxide has restored health to many people with cancer, arthritis, coronary heart disease, colitis, gum disease, herpes, hepatitis, childhood diseases and even AIDS. Ozone occurs naturally in snow and rain, from atmospheric ozone, and in mountain streams where rushing water is continually aerated. Lourdes water is fed by high altitude snow melt that absorbs unusually high quantities of ozone on its way from the upper atmosphere. The curative power lies in a few principles; spin and oxygen.

Adding spin to molecules of water heals the water, states Dan Winter in his film, "Sacred Geometry: The Unified Field." The molecules of water can absorb universal memory from spin. This idea is related to fractal and recursive chaos theory. Thus, water, its "matter," touches universal mind and heart. Winter has constructed a "sevenfold heart-shape braid" wherein water runs through seven dishes that are heart shaped, allowing a path of spin and pulsing to occur in the water. The water beats like a heart in the dishes it flows through, and each dish is in a ratio of the golden mean to the next dish. The water which arrives at the end increases germination quality and this method can cleanse sewage. This principle of purification and heightened "memory" is also created by "shaking" the very distilled Bach Flower remedies. The shape of a nautilus shell or the horn of a bull or cow also give spin for memory and purification.

The other principle is that benign microorganisms like our own cells require oxygen for health. Those cells which cause disease tend to be more primitive, having developed in ages when free oxygen was far less abundant. Our own cells are revitalized with oxygen while pathogens succumb to the high oxygen. Oxygen deficiency results in incomplete chemical reactions wherein wastes, toxins, and free radicals are left remaining—excellent precursors to cancer. Natural H_2O_2, or hydrogen peroxide, is found also in raw uncooked vegetables and fresh fruit juices. Hydrogen peroxide is found in mother's milk—is part of the immune system. It is found in the high Andes in a tree, the Taheebo, that holds oxygen in crystalline form in its inner bark. The bark has been used for centuries by the native peoples for health, and they don't get cancer. Dr. Christian Bernard, who performed the first heart transplant, takes hydrogen peroxide daily (in a very diluted and pure form) to decrease aging and arthritis. (There is controversy regarding hydrogen peroxide in different commercial forms which may actually produce free radicals—like certain fats and food preservatives do—which harm the body.) Hyperoxygenation via ozone or O_3 is used for AIDS and cancer patients by blood infusion similar to the process of dialysis. For lesser conditions, ozone may be used instead of chlorine to purify bathing water; one may bubble ozone through the water or pump air past an enclosed ultraviolet lamp.

Purifying blood via ozone is presently illegal in the U.S.A. The FDA does not approve. But freedom of religion does not preclude a journey to healing waters. And Lourdes is more than ozone. It is a faith in the heart.

North of Santa Fe is the "Lourdes of New Mexico," the El Santuario de Chimayo, where crutches are hung on the walls by pilgrims who have been cured by the healing mud in the chapel. Once a hot springs, many were drawn for healing in 1701, before the chapel was built in 1816. Sometime between 1850 and 1860, the young daughter of a villager near Chimayo heard a church bell ringing beneath the ground. She and her father began digging and unearthed a bell as well as a wooden statue of the Santo Niño. In the Land of Enchantment, there is little dividing line between the magical and everyday life—between God and the belly of the earth.

Chapter 6

The Serpent And The Sun

"If we kiss the snake on the tongue, if it senses fear, it will eat us instantly, but if we kiss it without fear, it will take us through the garden."

—Oliver Stone's film "The Doors"

On the Cabalistic Tree of Life, a serpent ascends in a spiral up the tree following the path of the sun. The serpent represents the hard path of evolution from matter to God. From the serpent-power to the Grail cup is the long wave of E-motion.[1] The serpent is part of Maya—an awesome illusion that Hindus take seriously as part of the path to Brahma. God may also arrive in a bolt of lightning from above, the tree quivering in cosmic light. The serpent earth energies and the solar energies are at opposite ends of the spectrum of life and psyche. Too much darkness is called Ahrimanic, and too much light is Luciferian. Both are outside the human realm. Yet, our consciousness and our future is a place of widened experience and sight. One may fly high into heaven and see glimpses of the All. Or else, one can rest languidly beneath trees, the sleepy afternoon entwined in branches, the reptilian slumber, its slow pulse, in the spine.

The Jungian author Marion Woodman once lectured on the negative reptile or lizard energy that results in too much or too little light and energy. A negative serpent pulls one down, a feeling of "I don't want to go to work, I'm too tired, I'm too fat!" versus a serpent energy moving too fast, doing more and more, producing at the cost of losing reflective creativity—like the dinosaurs of yore that sped over the landscape.

The secret to being human, however, is to be both on earth and in heaven, simultaneously.

In the Indian Tantric way of love, Shiva, the male Hindu god, sees the image of Shakti in his mind. He steps down from the heavens to meet her, Shakti, goddess of the serpent mystic fire, who lies coiled asleep at the base of the spine. Shiva, or Siva in Hindu tradition, is destroyer of illusions; is Time, Justice, and thus regenerative. His throat, dark blue, is adorned with a garland of human skulls around his neck—symbolic of immortality. On his forehead is a crescent, a third eye. He is often represented riding a white bull, and his hair is reddish. When Shiva approaches, enchanted, Shakti joyfully awakens, and rising up the spine, she embraces the sun. Uniting in tantra, a sensual mystical art of love, an expansion of consciousness occurs. Courting the five senses fully—in order to go beyond the five senses—is where the most sublime experiences occur.

Most of us have waited all our life for the wedding.

It takes preparation. Icarus, the young man in the Greek myth, flew too near the Sun, despite warnings from his father. His wax wings melted, and he plunged into the sea. Icarus symbolizes approaching the realm of the gods unprepared. There are female Icaruses. These are the solar-worshipping females. They deny the body and worship the sun. Their sun is a patriarchal one—the father aspect of our culture in America. A fixed sun is nothing like the feminine body. This sun is really a super-sun, a super-ego of parental and societal images. It is of appearance and not the inner divine sun—not a Shiva. It does not come down from heaven to meet her. Thus, it is really relentless. The feminine denied, Icarus females lose weight to fly. They vomit up the earth. They may eat everything up, looking for the mother. Food begins to have a magical quality, for it takes the place of the mother. (Digestion of food and of emotion use similar slow frequency waves—are consumed in a kind of marriage within the self.) Silly butterfly! In flight between sun and earth. In no man's land. Anorexics may finally feed off their own flesh, and die.

There is a ritual called the Celestial Burial, in which a lama will feed a dismembered corpse to vultures. For Tibetan Buddhists, this ceremony is a soul-releasing celebration for the reverence of all life. This ritual comes after a full life. But in rituals of addiction, like eating disorders, life is taken prematurely, the soul of one is never reflected properly, nor lived in the flesh; since there is no true courtship, one is merely sacrificed.

THE SINGING IS NOT REALLY SINGING
(for 1970s singer Karen Carpenter, who died of an eating disorder)

It is hard.
She is losing weight.
At zero, do all physical laws break down?
They shake her, "Eat!" "Eat!"
she gulps like a small star
her needles fall like broken shadows.

she feeds above earth, blue womb
nourished on light
the chlorophyll of noon

Do the parents love the body
of that child,
want to open her palms
let her go, silly butterfly?

Can we say what it is?
Our eyes are away every summer

we hear of air crashes
Icarus females
that fall into the sea,

was that her body that crashed?

How can it be fixed?
doors and flesh
a neurosurgeon coming down on the brain
like a deep-sea diver

after the second breath
father says, Once I had a little girl
he steps out into the dark snow to weep

what can she do?
she screams, I love you! I love you!
dances around her room
finds flowers for the parents

she almost sings like the flowers
the way mood is turning in the world

but the flowers are not really flowers
they are paints held to the knife
and the singing is not really singing
but a landscape full of hissing

she will be good
go to the closet
where she hates herself
try to fit the clothes

the parents wonder where the bruises
have come from, We have never touched that child

bruises make her think of light trying
to get out, the compass needle in the attic
barely trembling North
to the sea outside that is very slow
in an endless falling toward her.

Those with eating disorders are on an instinctual path to Shakti that goes aberrant because the crisis is not seen for what it is. At the physical level, the Shakti serpent is very particular about the food she wants, for she burns and purifies as she moves up the centers of the body toward the light brain. Grains, fruits, raw sugar, nuts, and ghee (clarified butter) are pure energy-type foods that are a good offering to her. And it is best to eat anything with enthusiasm, as many eating disordered people do—at least in secret. Such food and spiritual preparedness leads the way to the divine, although Jesus emphasized that it is not what one puts in their mouth, it is what comes out. It is enthusiasm for the divine that feeds.

I remember a young woman, age fourteen, who was a patient when I was working on an adolescent psychiatric unit. She was asked by a peer if she felt "life is too much." Very depressed, she answered, "No. Life is too little." I thought of Joseph Pearce's statement in his book, *Evolution's End*, when he wrote that at age fourteen or fifteen: "something tremendous is supposed to happen . . . a secret unique greatness in the self that seeks expression is supposed to happen, but doesn't."[1] Pearce thinks this is a time when new consciousness is developing in the young person, related to actual brain changes. During infancy and early childhood, mylenation, or sheathing, facilitates faster, more efficient movement of electrical impulses of the axons and neurons. But an odd thing develops and abstract thought enters when at age eleven the brain releases a chemical that dissolves all unmyleniated fields, removing 80 percent of the brain mass available at age six. Thus, around age eleven, formal operations begin. Words such as truth, beauty and virtue enter the conceptual vocabulary of the child. The light brain opens, which is responsible for all the great art, technology, architecture, science, profound compassion and divine love to be found in human beings. In young adulthood, more than just a case of hormones, there is a blossoming of the illumined and intuitive minds. The young person will have new loves of all kinds—love of music, drawing, dance, and science. An inquisitiveness about society, religion, great ideas, and the romancing of life emerges.

The mind is basically quiet in a child, whereas in a young adult, there is much inner dialogue. The Sun, Logos, begins to express, and also there is the subtle Kundalini, the Goddess of Speech. An inner Shakti-Shiva courtship. Too often, however, young people begin to lose heart, imagination, and a sense of inventiveness in the world.

Instead of exploring the enthusiasm and genius of their perceptions, their souls begin to resist their own impulses. The true impulses are not violent, addictive, or apathetic. Modern "narcissism" is an inability to dialogue humanly. In Bangkok, Thailand, teens live in monasteries for a number of months. The bliss and peace that is experienced is never lost. The crowded city of Bangkok is noted for its gentleness, serenity, and magic.

Resisting the true impulses to a full human life literally calcifies the self. Even by age six, the pineal gland is partially calcified because much resistance has already occurred. By age twelve, the thymus gland at the heart center, or chakra, calcifies. From the crown down to the root and sexual chakras, most of us calcify. In one's seventies, diseases crystallize around the former process, like the degenerative diseases wherein a hardening or frozenness of being is apparent, such as osteoporosis, hardening of the arteries, Alzheimer's, Parkinson's disease, and arthritis. If one is not calcified—so to speak—then one would emanate light out of the top of the head, as depicted in old icons of saints and yogis. The cobra breath, used in Tantra, activates the brain centers and chakra energy centers. Simultaneously, the seven chakras (the energy wheels along the spine) and the dormant cells in the cranium awaken. The spinal fluid, charged with psychic energy, transmits the impulse and opens the fields of each of the seven chakra worlds. The breath that brings the life force up the spine to the medulla, the hood of the cobra, is best used when one has first opened the cranium. It is best to descend down through the chakras from the fire in the cranium, and gently meet the cobra. To arouse the Kundalini serpent first from the earth and have her rise through an unprepared body and cranium can be a shock to the system, for the serpent will simply eat through the protective etheric webs which lie along the spine and between the chakras. Too much earth and aroused subconscient energies can muddy and distort the light. Physical and psychological disruptions can result; the serpent fire may actually burn skin and nerve endings. Mood swings like manic-depression, sleep disorders, and schizophrenic-like episodes are known to occur. The serpent energy may lock pain into any site of preexisting injury. One may feel intense heat and cold, or else a creeping sensation along the spinal column. One may go out of body and experience other dimensions. A premature Kundalini results when there is unpreparedness or resistance physically and spiritually. Transmutation is interrupted, and matter is mesmerized or bound by the serpent, a locking of energies that is like the war between the evil Egyptian god, Set, who stared into Osiris's eyes to bind his light. Kundalini is a universal energy and intelligence that may bind or free. It is a force that can burn the chaff; it can cure headaches, blood sugar problems, asthma, ulcers, high blood pressure, thyroid and other glandular problems/blocks. It increases intelligence and creativity. In manic-depressives, for example, the energy is creative in the aberrancy.

One may prepare all one's life for a Kundalini experience and it never happens. Others may open the way to the divine for us, the way pioneers opened the West. Sometimes it is grace.

When Jesus said, "Touch me not; for I am not yet ascended to my Father," (St. John 20:17. The Greek is "Do not cling to me."), he was in transition, neither fish nor fowl. Not yet the God. The recognition was that touching of the body might withdraw attention from the third-eye center, and place it in the lower extremities of the body, which would bring the energies down into the lower worlds before the divine has transmuted them. Having worked with people with schizophrenia, I've noticed they also say "don't touch" out of fear of confiscation, and schizophrenics talk about God incessantly.

The serpent energy may be terrifying—like a psychosis. In 1975, a sociologist stood on the Ohio Serpent Mound, a serpent and egg configuration invoking fertility, which weaves over hundreds of yards of ground. On a windless day he felt suddenly "the coldest, most abject terror I have ever experienced." There was no wind, yet the leaves crept unnaturally toward him rising and falling like footfalls. When fifteen to twenty feet away "the leaves flew together, swirling around him in dance."

> A leaf stalks with theatric light
> says please seal this bond
> for all precious time.

Kundalini fluid is a psychic fluid, a physical event that is actually the shadow of a spiritual fire. It is a reordering of reality. Thus, one must be rooted to earth and poised for heaven, as the wall carvings of Egyptian Pharaohs with straight spines, and feet emphasized, depict. The Tantric marriage between Earth energies and solar begins in the third eye, the seat of consciousness, the pineal gland which resides in the mid-brain (limbic system) weighing under a tenth of a gram. The pineal gland is regulated by sunlight and magnetic fields, thus it is in tune with physical places and cycles of light. The pituitary and pineal glands also function around DNA synthesis and aging. The light within the brain is created from the melanin molecule. (Melanin is reduced from melatonin, which is a neurotransmitter related to light and sleep/dream cycles.) The visuals we see with our eyes, and the light in dreams, is really internally created. The limbic system, the place of dream, ("limb" meaning to wrap around, like the dreamy serpent ascending the tree) has a direct neural connection to the heart which is equally saturated with the melanin molecule. The paintings of saints, avatars, and divine incarnations depict halos and shining hearts.

The psychic eye, the third eye, is violet. In numerology, violet is the number eleven, which stands for revelation.

I NAME A VIOLET

It is raining and you are not home
my fingers on the sill
have strayed from green
I cannot sleep

Blankness of walls and I wait
I hold a lamp there
some shadow hurts

A mist persists and I lie here
the bottom of a river thought
You love my tears
You love my tears Not.

Soon you will be home
I will open the door
a boundless field
for those are your eyes

I take a violet to you
name it a thousand stars

A manifestation of an awakening consciousness is the three-headed cobra that opens like a hood and is physically felt. The three-headed cobra is allegorical to the idea of three brains, the reptilian, mammalian, and the neocortex, all expanded into one consciousness. The serpent in the reptile brain is a survival intelligence, like the mountain climber who is slipping and knows thinking won't save him. The reptilian brain developed itself to "perfection" anywhere from 20-300 million years ago. The more open and less-programmed neocortex is newer, traditionally 100,000-200,000 years old. The second brain is the emotional, mammal brain, and the third is the light brain where visions, positive trances, bliss and liberation occur.

Gopi Krishna wrote of his own Kundalini awakening: "Suddenly, with a roar like that of a waterfall . . . I felt a stream of liquid light entering my brain through the spinal cord . . . then felt myself slipping out of my body . . . I was now all consciousness without any outline . . . bathed in light and in a state of exultation and happiness impossible to describe."[2] This brought on an experience of enlightenment. It "persisted always, even in his sleep." He was conscious in his sleep—a continuous lucidity. A Kundalini rising brings one to the summit, and one may see past-lives and the future. Clairvoyance is automatic. Divine love is understood.

Bliss-shock

She steps
into a lovely explosion

she sees into grass,
and behind treebark
she hears the sound
of the fathomless waterfalls

waterfalls absorb the exquisite
water of her feeling

the magnet night
draws out the stars

It is the whole body and mind that is transmuted. The physical shadow for Kundalini psychic energy is the cerebral spinal fluid which is found around the brain and spinal cord and distributed throughout the body. The first structure to be formed in the human embryo in the womb is the spinal cord. (The heart is the first organ developed.) The adrenal nerve endings climb the spine in the same double-helix pattern found in DNA. The basic seven chakras align with the endocrine glands, the root extending below the body, and the crown above it. These points are all energy transmitters that radiate energy consciousness out into the universe as well as draw energy in. The chakra wheels align with the spine, rotating in clockwise and counterclockwise directions. Energy is received and projected through them, and they are perpetually rotating. The first energy wheel is the root chakra which "roots" a soul to matter, or a soul to earthly existence. Then follows the sexual, solar plexus, heart, throat, pineal-third eye, and crown chakras. The crown chakra is where the thousand petalled lotus, the multiplicity in All, is perceived.

In her Book, *Coming Back*, Phyllis Atwater recounts a near death experience she had in which she viewed from space "two huge masses spinning at great speed looking like cyclones."[3] One was inverted over the other—the top cyclone spun clockwise, and the bottom one spun counterclockwise. The lower mirrored the upper. Where the "spouts" were touching came rays, and where the spouts were she saw all her lives past and future. I thought giant chakras, spin and memory, the eye of God.

The transition from life to life-after-death may bring enlightenment. A friend, Frankie Garcia, dying of cancer, asked that the "bright lights" in his room be turned off. But the lights were already off and Frankie's physical eyes were closed. (Was he in the "third eye," of the thousand suns?) He said with a smile, "Now I am in the audience with the people who know."

But in an earthly incarnation, we fragment so easily, into the illusory worlds. In general, as one descends the planes of consciousness, "There is," wrote Sri Aurobindo, "always a diminishing power of intensity, intensity of being, intensity of consciousness, intensity of force, intensity of the delight in things and the delight of existence."[4] The planes of consciousness—the model I allude to being Sri Aurobindo's—are the following:

The ordinary mind is a concrete mind, and a mind that fragments reality. It ironically refers to reality with great assurance, but since reality seems at this level subject to a thousand conditions, the ordinary mind retreats into a grayish light of familiarity. It experiences neither deep joy nor deep sorrow, as these emotions are tiny points of light, easily extinguished.

The higher mind belongs to philosophers, thinkers. There is more clarity and joy of longer duration. This is a cold, linear light, but not without humor. Its tool is logic and the teleological argument that circumscribes its reach. Unfortunately, the more brilliant lights that attempt to squeak through are either quickly concluded into a prejudged system or else promptly rejected, for the higher mind attends to that which it can explain. It begins to understand when it has explained—even to the point of explaining something away.

The illumined mind is an effervescent state, its ground being closer to spiritual and aesthetic being. The illumined mind is often swept with enthusiasm, and is inspired, to capture what is experienced as a muse, a wave from without, touching the mind. It is enthused—meaning "to be with the gods." It is the start of immortal feeling. Many in this state begin writing poetry, or expressing in the arts, in architecture or theoretical science. It is the start of supermind evolution.

The intuitive mind is one where one stands in a clearing in recognition of ultimate Being as there waiting, both light and dark as part of a general flash. It flies to the sun in an eternal instant. Artistic and religious imagery is put upon its forms—the lightning is drawn to it. Intuitive language is concise, versus the more opulent language of the illumined mind.

The overmind is cosmic, and rare upon the earth at this time. This mind produces revelations and the highest spiritual experiences and artistic creations. It sees large extensions of time and space, It is divine beingness to which one has access "in hours of grace."[5]

My husband had a dream of a flaming serpent in the darkest black and a voice said, "Christ is a flaming serpent." I thought of Christ descending into Hell while on the cross, and going through the densest of matter consciously, to reach the other side—immortality.

To go below the root chakra, the base ground of human being, and enter into antimatter, or antichrist, is a place only for a god of true love, for most souls would be in a corruption of the vital and lower energies, with a serpent that is only an impostor light.

> She starts with armfuls
> of meadow light
>
> her garment
> of joy
> her ringed world
> cantering
>
> even the sky is stunned,
> the sensitive blue speeds
> stem to unlit stem

Notes:

—The physical Sun has been determined to have a diameter of approximately 865,000 miles and a circumference of 2,773,000 miles, yet its actual body has not been seen.

—Our body's atoms were forged by another sun. The mother sun, a supernova that created us, was millions of degrees hotter than the Sun of Earth.

—The brain's limbic system is the emotional/cognitive structure used in dreaming and is involved with the immune system ("I" versus other memory) and the body's ability to heal itself.

—Ohio Serpent Mound has been specifically likened to Draco or the ancient dragon, or Python/Pythagoras. The site's prehistoric geo-astronomy incorporates the Sun, Moon, and stars related to the Egyptian mysteries of measurement of the heavens with the earth. The serpent is believed to be in the act of swallowing the sun, or disgorging an egg. One angle measure gave 6.66, the beast number of Revelation? See Rev. 12:4 wherein the Dragon sweeps one third of the stars from the sky. (Resource: *Ancient American* magazine, issue #18 1997.)

The Lost Feeling

It has been said that at the deepest layers of our unconscious lie not fantasy, but telepathy. Marc, my husband, awoke one March morning and told me of a dream he had about a huge, snake-like creature hiding in the house, how he and I were taking off the legs of the bureau, trying to find it. I then finished the dream with my imagination, and wrote "The Lost Feeling," although it could have been called, "God Looking for Us."

THE LOST FEELING

She notices Venus, bright as the key of a piano
gets up from bed, says to him
you've got to get rid of it
it's somewhere in this house, and it's huge
he grabs a deer rifle and walks down the hall
the sky is deep indigo
a massive log lies slanted on the house
gravity dragging space
Where did you last see it?
under the bed, it was huge
she begins removing drawers from the dresser
softly pokes at clothing
he is taking the legs off the bureau
let's look carefully, and keep our senses, dear

in the kitchen
his dusty flashlight moves corner to corner
checks behind the icebox
on the wooden counter is a row of brown eggs

he calls back to his wife, do you want me
to put the eggs in a cool place?

yes, put them back, I don't remember
leaving them out

he goes back to the bedroom, turns the corner
there it is on top of his wife
kill it, she says, as it slides off and under the bed

At first he is a little jealous, but then
she starts to cry, I hope it is gone tomorrow
he asks, Do you have any remorse? Well, she says
in a serious way, not that I'd want to undo
my birth and conception, but I know true love
does not end with a shove from behind
Come here, don't cry, he answers
maybe if we leave the door open
it will leave on its own. But isn't it better
she suggests, to at least know where it is?

She hears him quietly rummaging room to room
she straightens pillows on the bed, the white thin covers
reflect flatly against her eyes
she puts throw pillow to her chest, "any luck?"
No, where is it hiding? She thinks maybe it's scared
but she says, let's just sleep tonight, this is crazy
then he answers, I want to be with you. Yes, she replies
I understand, this is more real.

after awhile, she reads her magazine
what are you reading about?
astronauts that have returned from the moon
one has written poetry ever since
having seen an earthrise
one is fiercely selling military arms
another questions whether the Bible
was written on this planet,
that sounds like you, he smiles
one returned to become a Coors' beer distributor
but one has seen UFOs and has had a deep longing ever
since

Why are you getting up, sweet woman?
I need to check my clothes
she gets up and walks down the hall nude
towards the woods she hears a wooden chime
an ache and a sadness descend into her chest
what's wrong? Nothing, I think it's gone

she returns against the white wall
a shadow on a branch slightly sways,
what's wrong?
Just a shadow in the hall, but it's from outside
anyway, there was nothing in my clothes
I pushed back the couch, it was clear
Be with me . . . I want to be with you.

Notes:

He grabs a deer rifle, an old ego response. The indigo sky is psychic. The serpent is huge; how can it hide then? A subterranean consciousness. We see its tail end or shadow, as it slips between worlds. It drags down matter—gravity dragging space. The row of eggs—she doesn't recall leaving them out. Egg as creation, as resurrection, or perhaps cosmic egg laid on the primordial waters. But this is not one egg, for where we find one, we find a nest . . . ominous. She says, "maybe it will be gone tomorrow," but I ask, why not today? Her husband is momentarily suspicious, jealous. He asks, does she have any remorse? Because he doesn't know the serpent from Adam. And then the mere act of looking for the serpent— upsets it. From light, it recedes, an ineffable unconscious into the woodwork. Finally, she says, "kill it." She reads her magazine. It is her denial. The future and not this, not a serpent, maybe a UFO. One can tolerate the serpent in one's house, but not in complete visibility. The shadow is not from the branch, but on the branch. A guest? Our world is but its shadow—the falling skin. The ice-box is already old to most Americans, almost prehistoric.

Chapter 7

Serpents Of The Lakes

"Some people see a monster. We see improper metering, poor lens selection, and a total lack of composition."

—photography ad using famous Loch Ness photo

The debate continues about the Loch Ness Monster, the creature looking over the Scottish lake like a periscope. I wonder what the lake serpent sees when it views humanity—a total lack of composition? Lake serpents like the Scottish "Nessie" are a form of the serpent intelligence as elusive as the types that live on land, or in fire. Although lake serpents may be physically seen, they have not been proven to exist. Though they have been touched physically by a rare individual, no evidence other than the experience is taken away. Then, a watery hypnotic dissociation from it ensues, as if the experience is best kept veiled from us.

On April 14, 1933, a sighting of the Loch Ness monster was reported in the Inverness Courier newspaper. By the end of 1933 there were roads and picnic sites at the lake, enticing possible witnesses. Sightings, however, go back several centuries, and the description of the creature suggests that it is a vestige of a species that died out millions of years ago, closely related to the Plesiosaurus of the Mesozoic era. Thus, lake serpents like the Loch Ness creature have lived through several ice ages. Yet, its gravest danger was datelined in London, July 27, 1970, headed "Pollution Threatens the Loch Ness Monster."

Lake monsters have apparently been seen and even touched—but there is no hard proof. The Loch Ness types have left no skeletal remains, nor excrement. (Curiously, the bones of animals—deer, squirrels, raccoons, et cetera—are not easily found, despite countless ongoing deaths. Why are the woodlands and wild places not littered with bones? Some say it is because the animal wanders off knowing it will die soon and finds a very discreet, hidden place to die. Human skeletons are easy to find as death takes many of us unconsciously.) Nevertheless, lake serpents cause eerie states of mind. The twilight eel. They elude submarines with sonar and powerful searchlights. The water is murky with peat.

Near the famous loch of the Loch Ness monster, is a rock formation known as the Rock of Curses. Witches' covens have met here since prehistoric times. Perhaps these "witches" punch holes in the astral realm, conjuring up the serpent. The eyes glitter. The Loch Ness is salt-free and seldom freezes, because winter temperatures average around thirty-five degrees Fahrenheit, and so temperate conditions prevail. The Great Glen, of which Loch Ness is just a part (Findhorn is not far away, with its giant vegetables), is believed to be at least three hundred million years old, and it is the largest freshwater lake in Scotland. I have been informed that Loch Ness is thirty-seven miles at its widest, twenty-four miles in length—which is odd when one considers that length is longer than width! The lake walls go practically straight down. There are no islands. Much of the lake is seven hundred feet or more, which is deeper than the average depth of the North Sea.

Wherever the serpents are, their habits have been surmised in detail. There is little plant life within the peaty acidic water, so they must be eating fish. The menu may include brown trout, salmon, stickleback Arctic char, or sea trout. Fish have been found in the stomach cavities of the fossil remains of plesiosaurs, and there were many types of fish-eating plesiosaurs seventy million years ago. An ancient monster has a change of menu through the Ice Ages.

The New World has its monster also. Lake Champlain, once part of the Atlantic Ocean, lies between the borders of Vermont and New York—a day's drive from downtown Manhattan. The lake was "discovered" in 1609 by the French explorer Samuel de Champlain, who recorded, while actually on the lake, sighting a serpent-like creature that was about twenty feet long, thick as a barrel, with a head like that of a horse. The Iroquois Indians had already named the creature "the Great Horned Serpent." In 1988, Sandra Mansey and her fiancè, Tony, were picnicking at Lake Chaplain when, Sandra says, the lake "began churning" and she saw humps breaking the surface, gliding along, then subsiding. "It" then "gracefully" rose to the surface with arched, bending neck, weaving slowly up and down, in and out of the water, stretching about twenty feet. Sandra watched as it moved its head back and forth scanning. It would open its mouth and water would come out of it. It stared right at her. Sandra said she felt "oddly serene" but also that "I shouldn't be there; something I shouldn't be witnessing. It should be extinct, but I felt calm. It looked right at me, then it gracefully went down into the water." There are New York and Vermont resolutions to make the serpent of Sandra's sighting an endangered species. Is it not haunting and beautiful to put a creature on the Endangered Species List before it is even proven to exist?

At Salt Lake in Utah, seagulls glide over the lake in the midst of a desert. The ancestors of these gulls also were born in the desert. North of Salt Lake is another lake, Bear Lake, which is in green mountainous habitat. Legend has it that a serpent was pulled out in the 1880s—named "the Great Horned Serpent" by local Indians. Once these lakes were part of the sea—and will be so again when the floods return. Serpents entrapped by land will be let loose into the black years of oceans. Lake Titicaca in Peru once communicated directly with ocean. It was geologically pushed up to its high altitudes. Lake Titicaca has a species of sea horse, or Hippocampus. (The hippocampus in the midbrain is named for a structure that helps establish long-term memory in regions of the cerebral cortex.) This sea horse lived in the days of Incan sacrifices to the gods. UFOs are even seen darting about the area in modern times.

Do UFOs and water serpents have a common reality? Tom E. Bearden, a retired lieutenant colonel and systems engineer in the aerospace industry, has written of quantum psychotronic physics wherein "thought materialization" can create "a family of plesiosaurs in Loch Ness." He views UFOs as female mandalas (similar to Carl Jung's belief), and the late 1970s cattle mutilations as another feminine symbol, that is, the cow. These symbols of Mother Earth present as alien to us because we have cut them off.

I had a dream of standing in black water and in it was moving a black serpentine neck. Stepping back, the neck arose and there was a swan that fluttered gracefully over the water. A transformation, serpent into swan. I knew that it had once flown with the gods. But that not lasting, now here it lays its black-webbed foot, melancholic as the Swan of Tuonela.

SWAN

He sees a light, a pencil path
it slips over the lake
becomes swan

it presses a snowy silence
into the water
its graceful neck loosens the air
clarinet spray

it sings, it is dying
finished or unfinished
he is slowly reeling in
the swan, anesthetic as ice

it obsesses his heart
he goes to his room to bear it
damp feathers
blue and white muteness
let it go

he is full of holes
afraid to choose, what vase

and what aspect of flower
to place beside its breast

he is in the deep-knocked wood
silence and its decay
frozen creeks, branches . . .

Notes:

—A Templar, while being tortured by an inquisitor on February 13, 1310, spoke of the Kingdom of the Swan. He related traveling through time in a flying chariot, and spoke of a deep well of darkness through which one could attain immortality (black hole?) and reach unknown stars and empires . . . of an apocalypse between the forces of good and evil.[1]

—Some researchers surmise that the Loch Ness and other sea serpents may be ancient whales.

—The creatures of the oceans of the earth are only beginning to be known. Ninety-seven percent of the ocean's life and character is hidden in depths up to seven miles deep with immense pressures, wherein live creatures made of water (as only water is not crushed here) who feed on complete darkness and on the hot gases of volcanoes that spew heat and chemicals. Life begins here. On Europa, a moon of Jupiter, is an ocean deeper than Earths', and Europa is covered with volcanoes.

Chapter 8

Body Electronics Of Santa Fe

"And his disciples asked him, saying, 'Master, who did sin, this man or his parents, that he was born blind?' Jesus answered, 'Neither hath this man sinned, nor his parents, but that the works of God should be manifest in him.'"

–St. John 9:23

I heard the story of a minister who went to Nigeria and experienced a poor first reception with the people of the village. He prayed alone and wondered if he was doing the right thing, or was he simply a fool? He decided to try a second time and entered a building to speak, wherein the air was very hot. He thought that a furnace had been turned on, which would be an odd thing to have happen in the heat of Africa. He continued, however, to speak to the crowd, which was now curiously attentive to him, and seemed even spiritually moved. Later, the minister realized that there was not a furnace to be accountable for the heat in the building. The fire was of the spirit, a Kundalini that moved among the people.

Dr. John Ray, a naturopath, has given a series of lectures in Santa Fe on the power of Kundalini to heal the body and mind in the modern western world. By healing, Dr. Ray means mental and biological restoration wherein patients have had silver and gold fillings transmuted to perfect normal teeth, spinal fusions completely restructured back to normal with steel rods dissolved, and old infarctions of the heart healed to the point that no evidence of scar tissue remains. In addition, hearing has returned to deaf ears. Thousands of people in North America have had healings with Kundalini.

To prepare for a Kundalini healing, Dr. Ray focuses on visualization and unconditional love. He stresses that the fire of Kundalini can only work when combined with love. Proper nutrition, mostly raw vegetables and fruits, minerals and enzymes prepare the body. One's body, and even spine, may be wrecked and injured, wherein yoga is futile, but the heart must be pure and the body non-toxic. The central concept beyond love is that the structure of body is a manifestation of thought. One takes responsibility for thought patterns and transmutes on a mental level first. One must be able, mentally and in the heart, to experience all emotions from the standpoint of unconditional love. Resist not evil (St. Matthew 5:39). During a healing session, one will visualize violet on an injured area. Even an observer can project violet light to strengthen a person (visualizing black weakens). By using point holding on calcified areas of the body—injured areas that hold the memory of the injury like a crystal—the memory comes up along with the pain. One woman had the memory of the pain of the knife while under anesthesia. Another woman said, "I felt like a laser beam" when the fire moved into each vertebrae, burning calcifications. A burning, searing pain will begin to activate on the calcified areas. Also, point holders will discern a pulsation, the universal rhythm that activates all life. This pulsation, seventy-two beats a minute, is the universal pulse (not cardiac) in all life. By visualizing violet and experiencing all memories, pain and emotions with love, a healing can occur instantaneously.

The energy goes to the genetic level where deep thought patterns, pain, feeling, and memory reside. With a mastery of energies, one can overcome DNA, for we are creators from within and have free will. Studies such as palm readings are recognized as the external effects of the inner self. Lines may disappear on palms. Dr. Ray says he also sees changes in the irises of eyes; blotches dissolve at clock positions, and despite race, irises change in twenty-four hours from brown to blue in some cases. Part of the DNA pattern changes. This is a change in the nature of humankind. (Oddly, if one is under anesthesia, and for example, one's gallbladder is removed, the eye will record only a weakness in the area of the iris and blood vessels of sclera, but not that the gallbladder is missing, unless done so when the person was conscious!)

When one person heals, so may another. A child may heal while a parent is completing a healing crisis far away. A husband may heal a wife. Morphogenetic fields. Even more than genetic connections are soul connections where simultaneous healings occur. Christ's resurrection was a healing of mind and body in a huge way that opened the door to humanity, whom He would ask, "Do you Want to be healed?" (not everyone does) and He said, "these things I do, you will do more."

Why are we so unwhole? Dr. Ray states that in adolescence enthusiasm is squelched—the opposite of enthusiasm is unconsciousness—and the young person resists their own verve for life which creates calcification of the pineal gland. The illumined mind is thwarted from expression. Crystalline formations, which start up and continue through adulthood, also constrict the thymus gland. Cerebral spinal fluid, which is the physical shadow for Kundalini psychic energy, is also blocked. Cerebral spinal fluid is found around the brain and spinal cord and distributed throughout the entire body. Deficiencies in minerals and enzymes create calcifications that distort the flow of Cerebral spinal fluid. Dr. Ray gives specific directions to look indirectly at the sunrise five minutes a day, a reflective look and without any glass in between, to clear the pineal gland—for light is a nutrient.

One day at the beach, Dr. Ray experienced a Kundalini on the skin. His ankles began searing, burning out of proportion to the temperature on the sand. Then he was no longer John, but a Bedouin wandering in the desert for four or five days. Arriving at a tent, he knew the use of flaps for sun and cool breezes "for Bedouin tents are always cool." He knew the smell of camel. He later wondered if this was a soul or a genetic memory or past life. Or did it matter, as all time and selves are one. After this healing crisis, he tans but no longer burns as before.

Notes:

—A warning: Dissociation from pain/memory is an automatic protection, and opening to traumatic memories prematurely is simply a reenactment of abuse.

Chapter 9

Mars:
The Next Eden

"I wonder if all of astronomy, astrophysics and related science is not a protective decoy to keep us out of the 'real' universe until we are ready."

–Brian O'Leary, ex-NASA scientist,
from Exploring Inner and Outer Space

$\mathcal{T}$he question is: Will we ever fly-fish on Mars? For certain, revivification of Mars is being seriously planned. Slated for the year 2150, ample streams will run on the planet, and there will be non-salt carbonated oceans, a Mars Perrier. Let me explain. On the cover of Life Magazine, May 1991, is a picture of Mars with the headings "OUR NEXT HOME," and "MARS: Bringing a Dead World to Life."[1] The article inside sketches out in detail the plan to revivify Mars—to create an atmosphere and water supply wherein the planet can support and evolve life once again. The plan is to land humans on the planet by 2020, and by a concerted effort of the United States, Russia, Japan, Europe and other nations, our new home will be terraformed in less than two centuries.

It is good to familiarize oneself with the next man-made Eden.

A Mars day is similar to an Earth day in length. Seasons are about twice as long—a six month summer! (A Mars day is 24 hours and 37 minutes; a Mars year is 687 days.) In the middle of a Martian summer day near the equator under a bright creamsicle colored sky, the temperature may reach 10 degrees F, though usually never above freezing. But unfortunately, most of a Martian summer is not quite so frolicky, the summer night temperatures being minus 125 degrees F. This is comparable to Earth's Antarctica zones where minus 128 degrees F has been recorded as a low. Mars has a "warm" dusty southern summer season, but more usual is the colder dust-free northern season. (Surprisingly, the Hubble telescope reveals that Mars has a blue sky and white clouds.) Like Earth's, as the Martian North Pole goes through its summer, the ice cap diminishes. (The polar caps consist of frozen carbon dioxide and water). The question is, how does ice in sub-zero temperatures melt? Mars may be going through an Ice Age; its last interglacial change may have been as recent as 10,000 years ago, as is true on Earth. When the next warm period arrives on Mars, the planet will flow again with water. There are earthlings in high places who wish to artificially speed up the process. All the water on Mars is presently either frozen at the poles, or underground. But at one time, rivers flowed that were a thousand times larger than the Mississippi. The water of Mars contains a proton and also a neutron—a rarer form of water called "heavy water."[2] It exists beneath Mars' surface in huge reservoirs at an average depth of several meters. Mars was once warm and wet like Earth.

No known living organisms have been discovered on Mars. But then, in the early days of space exploration, satellites that were used around Earth gave readings suggestive that life could not exist on our planet—too little water vapor and oxygen to support life as we know it on Earth! Later, higher-tech probes did ascertain that we can exist here.

Mars is half the size of Earth, but its topography is gargantuan. One of its many volcanoes could be called Montana for its size. In the Tharsis mountain region sits the volcano, the Olympus Mons, at 90,000 feet—the highest known elevation in the solar system. Its top is 45 miles across, and it sits 15 miles above the surrounding plains. (Mt. Everest on Earth is 29,000 feet.) Below is a short version of the plan to revivify Mars, paraphrased from the Life article:

2015-2030: The first earthlings land in spacesuits. The atmosphere is thin as that of Earth at 130,000 feet—mostly carbon dioxide. Voices are deeper because sound passes through more carbon dioxide molecules, which are heavier. A base and various technologies will be set up, and experimental plants installed. The first step will be to alter the atmosphere to warm the planet, and melt the poles—the basics.

2080-2115: Puffy white clouds pile up; water pools in deep canyons. At minus 15 F, a tundra will begin in some latitudes. The population is up to 50,000. No more spacesuits. People can now use rebreathers; life is less cumbersome.

2115-2130: At 32 degrees F, evergreens and larches bud and a thin layer of organic soil will form. 250,000 people will live on the planet with nearly half born there.

2130-2150: Ample streams, with oceans carbonated and not yet salty. Rain will fall regularly and there will be several types of crops. Industries and boomtowns spring up.

2150-2170: One may finally breath unaided, though on a third less than Earth's 21 percent oxygen. Bigger lungs.

2175: It is the promised land of the twenty-second century. With plentiful raw materials, Mars finally financially repays. It even becomes a rich colony. Martian wildlife abounds.

A very promising article. Imagine a climb up mount Tharsis, a raft trip on rivers of Perrier. Join Martian Audubon Clubs. Name birds the way Adam did. Look for signs of ancient Martians—stone rings, serpent mounds, and caves with anonymous handprints. Enjoy the end of an Ice Age, a remineralization of our bones. Martian farms will flourish, the soil balanced and free of deleterious insects. Martians will grow up with their own music, art, and stories. Go to the opera where falsetto reigns, and Beethoven's Fifth is deep as an earthquake. Attend Martian rock concerts, electronic booms off massive rock amphitheaters. Go to the athletics games, spend a Saturday among pole vaulters and catch the sprinters, who dash off 100 meters in 5 seconds. Attend the ballet, ask, as Arthur C. Clarke did in his book, *Profiles for the Future*, "What, I wonder, will Swan Lake be like on Mars, when the dancers have only a third of their terrestrial weight?"[3]

Martians may well be more graceful than earthlings. They will have new life and hope. They will have two moons. Summers will be twice as long.

A paradise, but be warned. A mere two hundred years ago, North America was a paradise.

In August 1993, in Santa Fe, New Mexico, Apache artist Bob Haozous created one hundred buffalo sculptures, priced very low for art of that caliber. He did this purposely. He called his exhibit "The Vanishing Herd." Haozous pointed out that when the West was young, buffalo were a cheap resource, and that was why he was selling his buffalo sculptures at such a low price ($250 each). The statues did sell out almost in a day and then only white wooden stands remained in their rows. The gallery now seemed like "a cemetery as one walked through it," said one reporter.

THE SEA OF COLD

She asks, new from Earth,
do I wish life on fossil planets?
does the sea puff, only puff more white clouds?

a Martian booms, this is ivory!
his lungs working like light bulbs
Meet Moon Rocket and Raccoon,
these robots are programmed . . .

they deliver, are voice-activated;
they move and eat sand, locate
their own ores, recycle their own parts . . .

It's dry as a bone, she says, it's Mars,

I could easily faint.
She turns to Moon Rocket and Raccoon,
and asks, When do you know a thing is alive?

When we see replication.
We'll take over the whole friggin' world.

We are waiting for an order,
says Moon Rocket. She looks up, says, bring almond oil
and peppermints, and a cigarette,
this is one lonely pit, she says reaching
for a light.

Raccoon says, We can move sand
to your tastes, carve aesthetic dunes,
Moon Rocket says, we are waiting for an order.
Yes, she says faintly, my confidence
seems to have failed, see there, she points
far off and away, the peaks, the ocean,
the peculiar white light

you see, she says,
every heart has its sea front,
its outpouring of salt and water,
its Beethoven and white whale.

We are waiting for an order.
I know, darlings, she says nervously,
I mean, this sea front is a great vast thing,
very cooling to blue eyes and white skin,

but she has started to faint, and cannot give an order
for she has fallen into the Sea of Cold
where tiny bones take an infinity to sink.

An ancient sea once existed on Mars, and near it is what is now
called The City. The City is located on a northern desert called
Cydonia, and includes the D&M pyramid, a tholus or mound, the
cliff, and the Face.

In 1976, the unmanned Viking spacecraft sent back a photograph from Mars of a 1.5-mile-long humanoid face staring straight out into space (2.5 km. long and 350 meters high). The Face has been studied by engineers, physicists, art historians, cartographers, architects, anthropologists, and theologians. Computer-vision techniques that derive three-dimensional views—shape from shading—from different perspectives and under different lighting conditions, point highly to artificial construction and not a natural phenomenon. The Face is bilaterally symmetrical and non-fractal, meaning artificial. It has a helmet headpiece, and a combination of lion and hominid can be viewed in it. The Egyptian Sphinx is similar in having the body of a lion, and a helmeted head of a man. The humanoid shape may be the ancient Hindu God, Lord Hanuman, a monkey god, symbol of service to God—a higher aspect of the monkey which is otherwise associated with mischievousness, chatter, maliciousness, gossip and deceit.

Zecharia Sitchin, in his book, *Genesis Revisited*, writes about the communication between Mars and Earth in ancient times: "Was the purpose, as the Egyptian text suggests, to send the 'message from Heaven' to the Sphinx on Earth, a 'command' according to which the gods acted, sent from one Face to another Fair-of-Face?"[4] Cairo, by the way, close to the site of The Great Pyramid at Giza, was originally called "El-Kahira," from the Arabic El-Kahir, which means "Mars." Thus, "Cairo" means "Mars."

Dr. Richard Hoagland, founder of the "Mars Mission," presented a talk to the United Nations on the monuments of Mars on February 22, 1992. A former NASA consultant, Hoagland explains that The Face and the D&M Pyramid were not placed haphazardly on Mars. Their orientation is in alignment with sunrise at solstice time on Mars. The entire City complex is based on artificial intelligence.[5] The complex replicates Avebury in southern England in its tetrahedral mathematical relationships. The D&M pyramid is a five-sided figure that is 500 meters high, and has internal mathematical constants that are tetrahedral. Ancient artifacts on earth are also based on tetrahedral mathematics—the Great Pyramid at Giza, The Sphinx, the mounds at Avebury, Stonehenge, and the pyramids of Mexico City and Peru. Some of the modern crop circles also display tetrahedral mathematics.

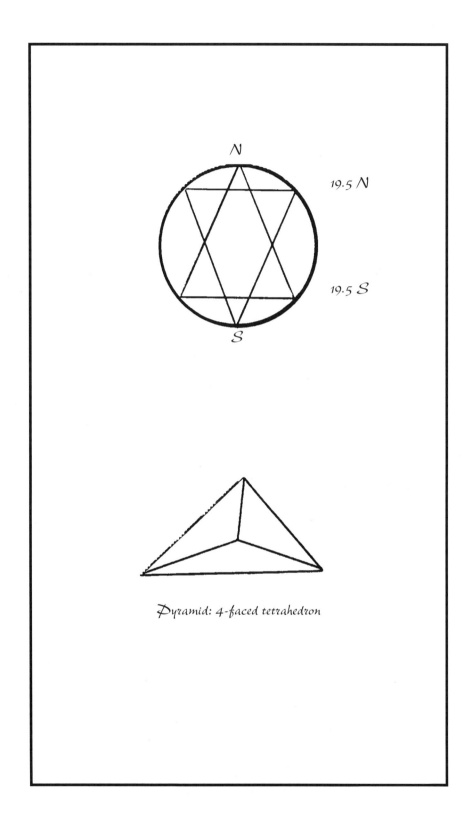

Pyramid: 4-faced tetrahedron

The tetrahedron was one of Plato's solids. What is its significance? Visualize two tetrahedra interpenetrating inside a sphere, not as a literal physical structure, but as a physics.

Note that the tips of the bases touch at key latitudes on the sphere planet—19.5 degrees north and 19.5 degrees south. The apexes of the tetrahedra touch at the north and south poles.

Dr. Hoagland points out that great "upwellings and downwellings of energy occur at 19.5 North and South latitudes on massive spheres." Jupiter's Great Red Spot (the permanent storm), Neptune's dark spot, the Sun's flaring sunspots, and Earth's largest active volcano, Mauna Loa in Hawaii, are all proximal to the latitudes of 19.5 north and south. At 19.3 north is the Olympus Mons, the largest volcano on Mars. By rotating the model above, magnetic fields, or energy ley lines which surround planets like a web, can be discerned from the inner tetrahedral model. This concept was taught in the mystery schools of Egypt and Greece.

Megalithic monuments based on tetrahedral mathematics were once used to control the electromagnetic energies of nature. The earth's ley lines begin and end with the Great Pyramid at Giza. The Atlanteans, and later the Egyptians, wore metallic head dresses, and woven metal scarves with threads of gold which hung down their shoulders, for protection from the strong electromagnetic field of the Great Pyramid.[6] The Egyptians topped the Great Pyramid with a ball covered with a plate of polished gold in a scale-like manner, and as the Earth turned, shafts of light were reflected in all directions. Several thousand years later, this metal ball with scales of gold has disappeared, along with the pyramid's white alabaster coating.

Rotation is a concept important to tetrahedral physics. Rotation, and especially high spin states, add "memory" in sacred geometry or in modern chaos mathematics. In Newtonian physics, only non-rotating objects are measured, but virtually everything in the universe and its atoms spin, rotate. That changes everything. Balls with spin go faster and farther, and fall faster than balls without spin. Objects in hyperspin and rotation can hover frictionlessly, like superconductors. There is no explanation for this in conventional physics. When a massive sphere rotates, energies and phenomena from higher dimensions will manifest. Jupiter, the fastest rotating of the planets (its day is nine hours) and the largest, has super-hurricane force winds that exceed 360 kilometers per hour (216 mph.) at the Great Red Spot—an especially huge anti-cyclone. The Sun is "less a chained hydrogen furnace," Hoagland explains, and more a "hyperdimensional portal" emitting energy from an infinite source.[7] The spinning Fatima sun is more understood, I think, when seen as a sun behind the Sun. That is, the physical Sun normally seen is actually a shadow projection of a higher dimensional body.

There is no current explanation for Saturn's rings, which span 171,000 miles, but are scarcely 60 feet in width. Hoagland suggests that they are higher level ripples in space-time created by Saturn's massive rotation. The rings may be a literal visual link between the third dimension and higher-dimensional reality. The sound of the rings may also be a link between dimensions. The emissions of the rings has been recorded, and sound, to me, like an oscillation of Tibetan bells. Is this Plato's idea of the "music of the spheres"?

Modern physicists, like John Worrell Keely, are developing free energy models based on "tetrahedral virtual rotation."[8] Using the MRA, or Magnetic Resonance Amplifier, energy is rotated relative to the harmonics of different frequencies. Rather than using physical energy to rotate a mass, the MRA uses resonance to rotate energy. Beyond the three physical dimensions is energy that can be tapped free at resonance, although the energy does vary locally, being more accessible at "power spots." The energy is more available at sunrise and sunset when the earth's magnetic fields increase. Energy in resonance, or harmony, is also less polluting and wasteful. Crystals may be used, and in the latticework of quartz silicon one can see the shapes of tetrahedrons.

Much has been learned about the physics of large spheres, and that artificial intelligence may have left its mark beyond Earth. Mars is the obvious next step for humankind, but there have been many delays in arriving there. In 1988 the Soviet Union sent probes to Phobos and Mars. The unmanned Soviet spacecraft called Phobos 2 arrived in the orbit of Mars in January 1989. Its goal was to transfer to an orbit that would make it fly close to the Martian moonlet Phobos and to explore the moonlet, placing instruments on it. When Phobos 2 aligned itself with the Phobos moonlet in March 1989, the Soviet mission control center acknowledged a sudden communication problem and reported that the spacecraft was lost for good. But, seconds before they lost contact, a photograph of an unidentified object on the Martian surface was taken. A few days earlier the "shadow" was recorded as being 16 to 19 miles long, called a "thin ellipse," a "phenomenon" 12.5 miles long, and was concluded to not be a shadow of Phobos or debris. Dr. Becklake of England's Science Museum described it as something between the spacecraft and Mars and stressed that the object was seen by both optical and infrared camera. He said that the Soviets saw "something that should not be there."[9] Many have asked, was this Star Wars?

In September 1992, the Mars Observer was sent to take pictures of the planet, but NASA decided to black out many of these shots; citizens were not allowed full disclosure.

In August 1993, new pictures of Mars were to be taken. However, the Mars Mission lost radio contact with the Mars Observer when a probe broke off mysteriously, so close to getting into orbit. Then the Ballistic Missile Defense Organization, formerly the "Star Wars" project, was asked by civilian space officials to determine if a fleet of fifteen small craft on an "emergency mission" could be prepared soon to land on Mars.[10] Collaboration with Europeans and Russians was mentioned, so why the emergency? Who else is there?

Notes:

—The Face on Mars may be 500,000 years old.

—In the February 1996 issue of *Science News* (Vol. 149, No. 5, p. 71) is a report that the Hubble Space Telescope photographed a huge elliptical "satellite" orbiting Saturn's rings. In a later photo, it disappeared. Two other bright objects were seen in 1995. NASA scientist Dr. Norman Bergrun said, "They have a tendency to hide." Dr. Bergrun's book, *The Ring-Makers of Saturn*, discusses a cigar-shaped craft in the rings, photographed by the Voyager. Apertures were even visible on this craft.

—Black holes, or collapsed suns, rotate at a million miles an hour.

Chapter 10

The Star Tetrahedron
&
The Merkaba

To see from an angel's point of view, start with the forms of sacred geometry. Sacred geometry has been referred to as the "sacred motions of spirit in the void." In Genesis it is the spirit of God over the face of the deep. It is the Morphogenetic structure behind all things in reality—on Earth and in heaven. As Genesis began in the mind of God, so can the world begin in a simple meditation. Begin with the Merkaba:

The Merkaba is a space-time vehicle (Egyptian/Hebrew). The word Mer denotes counter-rotating fields of light; Ka is spirit, Ba is body or reality. The whole configuration rotates as it moves through space. (The electrical field is moving in a wave, and the magnetic field is moving at ninety degrees to this wave; the whole electro-

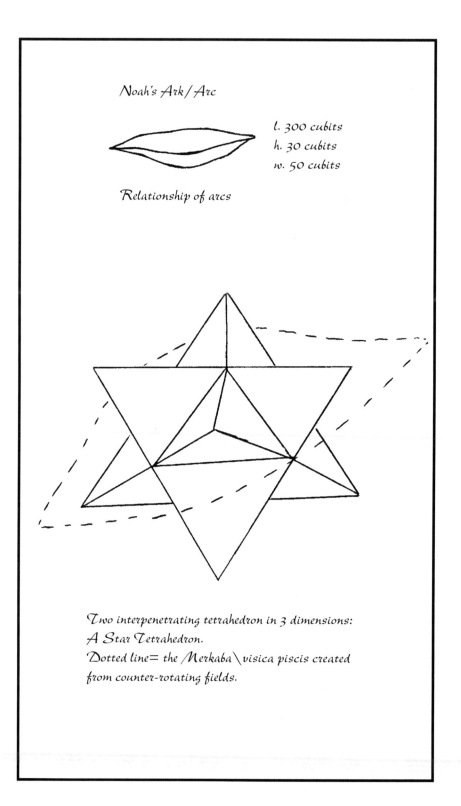

Noah's Ark / Arc

l. 300 cubits
h. 30 cubits
w. 50 cubits

Relationship of arcs

Two interpenetrating tetrahedron in 3 dimensions:
A Star Tetrahedron.
Dotted line= the Merkaba \ visica piscis created
from counter-rotating fields.

magnetic energy, or light, rotates as it moves through space, creating a force field, the Merkaba, which looks like a UFO.)

In this meditation, one visualizes drawing breath/prana through the fontanel and through the root chakra via a column that runs through the center of the body. This is the axis upon which the star tetrahedrons counter-rotate. The force field created by this rotation is called the Merkaba, which tunes one to higher states and amplifies thought and intention.

All but the last breath is now on the Internet. (The author suggests one find a flesh and blood teacher instead of the Internet.) The last, the eighteenth breath, is not taught. When a student is ready, their higher self will give the experience.

The Merkaba meditation is in the service of love, so there is a built-in protection—only with a pure heart can it start up. (However, an "external" Merkaba may be engineered without unconditional love, such as a UFO, or the evil 1943 Philadelphia Experiment, which was devised to make ships invisible to radar by changing space-time. United States crew members were welded in space-time to the ships' structure, some lost forever in an elsewhere dimension, and many insane.)

At the fifteenth breath, the star tetrahedrons take off from their setting at one-third the speed of light. A disk approximately fifty-five feet in diameter forms around the body at the level of the base of the spine. This is the Merkaba energy matrix which is described as being in the shape of a "flying saucer." At this point in the meditation, the Merkaba is unstable; it wobbles slowly. Thus, the seventeenth breath is used to speed one's fields to nine-tenth the speed of light for stabilization. (The three-dimensional universe is tuned to nine-tenth the speed of light; every electron in the body rotates around every nucleus at nine-tenth the speed of light.) At the eighteenth breath and beyond, one vibrates to the speed of thought which is faster than the speed of light. With the eighteenth breath, you disappear for a while. You are in the frequency of the fourth dimension and beyond. You may even bilocate, like Padre Pio or Sai Baba (multidimensional humans). One experienced student did the eighteenth breath and found himself very, very deep inside the Earth. He sensed it was Antarctica. Men in uniform who were eating in a mess hall, looked up surprised at his presence. Then he returned to his meditation spot.

In the Book of Revelation, an eagle takes the woman into the wilderness for a time on wings that rise above the physical condition. The woman has relief from the "serpent" (or double helix DNA) and flies into supernature.

One might deduce that transdimensional travel would be too accelerated or violent for the human body. There was the concern once that humans would not be able to breathe or stay intact riding in an automobile or plane. Before automobiles and aircraft, was Noah's ark or arc. The Old Testament gives the proportions for the ark, a Merkaba, or vesica piscis. A Merkaba, or Noah's Ark, has key physics properties. Spin a vesica piscis/arc clockwise and it obeys Newtonian physics in that it spins clockwise until it slows down. But spin it counterclockwise and it oscillates, stops, then begins rotating clockwise. Newtonian physics cannot explain this. A boat has been actually built in proportion to the ark of the Old Testament. A man took the vehicle through some rapids for an experiment. To bystanders, it appeared that the craft arced way up and over the waves—not darting through them as common sense expected, and the boat was whipping violently. It appeared the man would be severely hurt. But the man said he experienced the ride as smooth, and was unharmed. Did Noah "arc" in a similar kind of space-time vehicle through the Great Flood? (The Merkaba also manifests as "wheels within wheels" to Ezekiel; and as a fiery chariot to Elijah.)

In *Journeys Out of the Body*, Robert A. Monroe began initiating out-of-body experiences by rotating ninety degrees. (Each dimension is ninety degrees or perpendicular to the next.) After a vibration he would turn another ninety angle and enter a portal to another body.[1] This could probably continue forever. Monroe saw in one journey, a huge spaceship between Earth and our moon at about 50,000 miles above the surface of this planet. It appeared stable, "a nonhuman construct," gray in color, a long slender conical shape with a hemispheric dome at the widest end, and the other end was somewhere in the distance at least several miles. It appeared "motionless." Its origin, Monroe was told by an entity while out-of-body, is of our physical universe, but "not necessarily of your time reference."[2]

I wonder if the living Earth's breath could produce a Merkaba around her body, a huge space-time vehicle? Perhaps such a Merkaba can create crop circles—whorls of counter-rotating wheat and barley—especially if it starts to wobble between dimensions. If it starts to wobble, our planet will be stepping up in vibration and consciousness.

Notes:

—Charles Sherburne, a fireman, was curious as to what Noah's ark really was. He worked mathematically with the notion that the ark could be viewed as a relationship of arcs. That is, 50 cubits to 300 cubits is a one width to six lengths ratio and may be seen as an arc. A physical model of the ark was found to follow identically the figure-eight movement of the sun across the sky (really the earth's movement, or arc, around the sun). The ark model also arcs around oncoming waves differently than conventional ships, slipping around waves that normally crash over a ship. Sherburne refers to "cyclic geometry" as a new realm of understanding about Noah's ark.

—The frequency of the earth is speeding up. Schumann's resonance is a physical subsonic frequency of the planet Earth that has the same bandwidth of frequency as our brain and heart, and was first thought to be a human being when scientists detected it. This zero to forty-eight Hertz is also related to geological plate tectonics. The earth's resonance has been at 7.83 (theta-alpha boundary) but has increased in the last few years to 8.5+Hz (approaching 13 Hz). If the Earth's frequency increases, so do we, for we human bodies are within the larger body of earth. While the frequency of Earth is speeding up, its magnetic field is decreasing, approaching zero. With less magnetic "shield effect" thoughts/feelings may manifest/mirror back quicker. Information may come in floods.

—The DNA molecule is made up of a series of genes or units called nucleotides. DNA may be better understood as scalar wave antennae that organize the plenura or morphogenetic fields into holographic universes.

—DNA antennae communicate per energies passed from one portal position to another at the ninety degree angle. This shift is like that from before birth into an earthly soul, or from an earthly soul back to spirit after death. A merkaba meditator pointed out in class that if one watches films of the human ovum at conception, there are usually exactly twelve sperm oscillating around the sperm that enters the egg. It is as if they "hold the space" for the one that does enter the ovum, which appears to be done through an interdimensional portal. No penetration of the ovum can be seen in the third dimension. The sperm have "intent" and finally one of them will "jump," enter the ovum. The ovum is a container and is not "penetrated" or "broken"—we just assume that, as Newton assumed the universe operated on non-rotating and non-oscillating principles. (Sources: Drunvalo Melchizedek/Flower of Life Workshop and Kevin White Eagle/Mer Ka Ba instructor.)

—In 1513 Turkish Admiral Piri Re'is had a map of Antarctica showing the continent in a relatively ice free state. Antarctica has been covered with ice approximately six thousand years and only "discovered" in the nineteenth century. Antarctica was named "Insula Atlantis" on a seventeenth century map that correctly depicted the contour of the continent. The Piri Re'is map of the coast of Antarctica (as Antarctica appeared 5,000 to 15,000 years ago) is as accurate as any aerial map and uses an ancient form of spherical geometry.

Chapter 11

Sacred Sites:
Inner And Outer Space

"He stretcheth out the north over the empty place, and hangeth the earth upon nothing."

–Job 26:7

"Oh my dove, that are in the clefts of the rock, in the secret places of the stairs, let me see thy countenance, let me hear thy voice."

–Song of Songs 14:5

I have heard there is a planet named Reath, an ultimate physical world where Eden exists. Its purpose is to show creation that it is possible to have Heaven in the physical. But one can have only one lifetime on Reath. Adam had only one life in Eden. We are always trying to get back to Eden—a place where we fit in the cosmos, and where God is a physical presence walking in the garden.

Temples and sacred buildings were once built by humanity as power spots between the energies of Earth and the cosmos. They amplified natural energies for fertility, healing, and prophecy. In modern times, public places like churches, state capitol buildings and old city parks may have vestiges of an ancient need for physical settings to be a place where heaven and Earth touch through architecture, gardens, fountains, special foods, ceremonies and commerce. Such centers of civilization can be a haven for human intermingling of ideas, for the politic, or for the curiosity and joy of observing other human beings. The poor, the elderly or simply lonely can find peace and healing in public places. Monuments stand like a cool shade.

CEREMONY OF PIGEONS

In a park, a woman
lunches in the shade

pigeons, cool as pennies
on a tree
alight

onto a cloth
of the palest peach

she sets out tea and loaf
a ceremony for love
passed away

she puts crumbs
saucer in air

the pigeons consume
it, her pain
as if it were fruit

from the park, the city
their flight to her
is beautiful as march

they wait in trees
like old clothes
they stir like tin cans
between buildings

they will not vanish

Perhaps the most touching monument in the United States is the Vietnam Veterans Memorial in Washington, D.C. Fifty-eight thousand soldiers died in Vietnam; each soldier's name is inscribed on a reflecting black surface. As one approaches the wall, one's own reflection is in it, and the touch of fingers and hands over the names honors and beautifies the structure and the visitor. The wall's simple eloquence was designed by a young art student, Maya Lin, who was much criticized regarding the abstractness of the design, and the fact that she is Asian-American. But few complaints have arisen from the families who actually lost sons and brothers.

Ancient sites were aligned to heaven and Earth via their sacred geometry—a geometry inherent in the earth, the cosmos and the human body. The British inch, for example, is a measure of the earth, being equal to three grains of barley corn end on end. The measure of the speed of rotation of the vault of heaven is a natural astronomical cycle—1000 pyramid cubits a second. (A pyramid inch is 1.00106 of our inches. The sacred cubit is 25 pyramid inches.) Geometry means "measuring the earth." The human body is in resonance with Earth and cosmos. Sacred buildings reflected this relation with the golden mean or golden section, a proportion or ratio seen in nature, derived from a series of root triangles produced by compass from a double square and its diagonals. The carvings and art symbology on the walls of ancient buildings were sacred proportions to be incorporated in the mind's eye. The French painter Nicolas Poussin, (1594-1665), having visited the Roman temple, the Maison Carree in Nimes, France, wrote of the relationship between architecture and the human body: "The beautiful girls (you) will have seen at Nimes will not, I am sure, delight spirits less than the sight of the beautiful columns . . . since the latter are only the ancient copies of the former."

In recent years, there has been a proposal in the astronomy world, wherein some astronomers want to replace the light-year with the yottameter.[1] The yottameter is something one must look up in a book, whereas the meaning of a 100 million light-years is intuitive (and implies at once that it takes 100 million years for a galaxy's light to reach us, and that it is 100 million light-years distant). The new system would say that same galaxy is 10^{24} meters or one yottameter. How would Einstein have fared trying to visualize a yottameter, and not a light beam in his imagination, when he was discovering his theory of relativity? Instead of intuiting a light beam measurement which he "saw" in his mind, he would be left paging through texts of artificial numbers. A similar debate took place during the time when the Constitution of the United States was drafted in the 1780s. A new decimal system of measures was being endorsed based on the French system. Thomas Jefferson opposed the decimal system because time as a measure was left out.

On June 21, 1994, there was a "clash between hippies and British police at Stonehenge."[2] The police said touring hours were over while the hippies stated it was solstice, sacred time, and they wanted to stay for the experience, dream bluestones.

Megalithic circles like Stonehenge radiate energy fields. One may find delight or else be too charged. Stone sites can emit ultrasonic sounds when the sun is up in the morning and hits the stones. The stones light up like neurons, and some emit a shock at the touch.

Ancient stone rings and sites are also associated with psychic phenomena, UFOs and peculiar light. Such spooky phenomena may be in part what is experienced when one approaches high energy that is connected to the collective unconscious. Such a place of high transforming energy is in Jerusalem, where an occasional tourist enters a brief intoxication from the surrounding land and city and begins to believe he or she is the Messiah, or Mother Mary, King David, or Satan. The tourist often begins looking for locusts and wild honey in the outer wilderness. Members of the Israeli army are familiar with the syndrome. The army routinely and gently ushers these casualties (who are easy to discern, since they strip off their tourist garb and wrap bed sheets around themselves) to the psychiatric hospital, Kfar Shaul, on the northwest edge of Jerusalem. The stay is usually brief. Curiously, ninety-five percent of those under the Jerusalem spell are white Protestant Europeans and Americans. Protestants seek a direct contact with God and are at risk of being consumed by the unconscious more fully, as the ego has no intercessor. The first sign that a tourist is entering the Jerusalem syndrome is "a falling behind the tour."[3]

Sites alter perception. At Rollright stone circle outside Oxford, England, four official surveys resulted in four different totals for the number of stones. The estimate is still only "about" seventy. Quartz crystals are prominent at ancient and sacred sites. Crystals are extremely hard, and are virtually ageless. Crystals store memory.

Crystals are used in modern computers and watches. The lattice structure of crystals is very similar to the human molecular cell structure. (Hormones are made of crystals; hormone means "messenger.") Australian aborigines will initiate a young shaman by sewing a crystal into the initiate's belly that was used by a shaman that died, to transmit knowledge.

Ancient knowledge has been transmitted by crystal in the form of crystal skulls. While holding memory, quartz also "grows," or expands one-tenth of one percent a year every year. Frederick Mitchell Hedges and his daughter, Anna, thought they found a link to Atlantis when they discovered a crystal skull in a Mayan ruin, named Lubantuum, in 1919. The jungle was then British Honduras, now Belize in the Yucatan. The Mitchell-Hedges skull is thought to be that of a woman with oriental or Mongoloid features between the age of 17 and 20. One theory is that the skull is at least 12,000 years old, and was handed down to Mayan priests by Atlanteans, because the Atlanteans are the only ancient civilization believed to have had such ultra-advanced technology.[4] The clear quartz crystal is still beyond duplication by any modern technology. The internal lenses, light pipes and prisms are of stunning precision, and anatomical accuracy, except that suture marks which should be on top of the skull are absent. There are no instrumental markings. It weighs 11 lbs. 7 oz., is five inches tall and wide, 7 inches long. The skull has a prism which directs light from beneath the skull and out the eyes. Those peering into it report imagery of past scenes, including ancient temples, the sound of bells and human voices in a choir-like effect. Some enter trances, or see their thought manifest later.

The Mitchell-Hedges skull is the most intricate, but there are other crystal skulls. A southern France skull called "The Skull of the Light of Christ" has been connected to the Knights Templar. The Berlin skull was in Gestapo possession during World War II and was supposedly taken to Italy in the 1980s, perhaps to the Vatican. There is the British Museum Skull, but it was taken out of view in the late 1960s when hippies and flower children stationed themselves around it for hours and days on end.

A site covered with quartz is New Grange in England, built about 4000 B.C. When the sun rises at winter solstice, a ray of sun slowly inches back to a chamber 100 feet from the entrance. The light beam illuminates the back chamber for only 17 minutes. In the chamber is a recumbent stone with a triple spiral with three goddesses. The goddess waits in cycles of nature, waits as winter must, for the fresh struggle of spring; the solar god arrives with light to find her.

Notions of fertility are commonly invoked among ancient sites, as by the symbol of egg and serpent. In England, the huge mound of Silbury Hill near Avebury (thought by some to be the "Shakti of the World") covers five acres, is 130 feet high, and "uncoils across a thousand feet to grasp a sphere in its mouth."[5] The egg is birthed out of the serpent time, or strangely, Greenwich Mean Time near Silbury Hill. I find it an evocative coincidence that the mound of Silbury Hill is so near on the globe to Royal Greenwich Observatory, which is the site from which all time zones and all longitudinal measurements east and west around the world are made. The Observatory is in an inner borough of London, England. It is the location of the meridian of zero degrees longitude.

To see like a god through stone, this is what some ancients attempted. But Yahweh asked Job, "Where wast thou when I laid foundations of the earth? Declare if thou hast understanding!" (Job 38:4). To understand the foundations of Earth, the ancient Mayans, in a bloody ceremony, would throw children down a sixty-foot-deep well, and if any survived, they were to tell what the gods said down there.

With tons of stone and cosmic intelligence, the Great Pyramid at Giza measures the external world via its inherent geological mathematics manifested in stone, its astronomical alignment. The interior of the Pyramid initiates inner space; it is a temple where one may awake to one's own immortality. In the past, initiates would lie in a great stone sarcophagus for three days and experience the body as something one can slip in and out of without death. One would see the All behind the All.

The word "pyramid" means "amid the fire." The Great Pyramid is thought by conventional scholars to be at least 4600 years old, built around 2613 B.C. to 2494 B.C. The pyramid's mass is thirty times the Empire State Building and twice the volume. In its original highly polished state, it shone in the sun with rainbow colors. If seen from the Moon, it would have appeared brilliant as a star on Earth. (Presently, the only human made structure visible from outer space is the Great Wall of China).

The Great Pyramid is in the center of all the land area of the earth (displaced slightly by a proportion of the golden mean). It measures the Sun's distance from the earth (93,000,000 miles) by a number built into its base. (The Greeks thought the Sun was 10 miles distant in 500 B.C. Later they adjusted the figure to 2,000 miles.) The Great Pyramid measures the mass of the earth, approx. 6.6 x 10^{21} tons. It accurately measures the rotating earth traveling in its orbit around the sun counter-clockwise at the speed of 66,600 miles an hour. It also aligns with the Pleides, Sirius, and Orion in meaningful astronomical ways. (The three pyramids on the Giza plateau are in alignment with Orion's "belt" and geometrically enter the heart of Orion via the golden mean spiral. New stars are born at an unusually high rate in the Orion star system.)

The Pyramid is inherently close to the English system of measurement—not a metric system, but rather the ancient cubit and megalithic yard: 2.72 ft. It is also based on pi—the ratio between the circumference of a circle and its diameter. (In any size circle, pi is always 3.14159. Pi has never been ascertained to its finality—even up to 5,000 decimal places and written out to over two billion digits. Pi is considered one of the transcendental numbers.)

The Great Pyramid sits over a pit far older than itself. The pit (and the tunnel to it) is associated with the fourth dimension, where one's thoughts manifest back quickly. This can be terrifying for anyone, ancient or modern, and many have died. Thus, the Egyptian government has blocked off the ancient pit. Tourists, especially, are not prepared for the Great Pyramid's mysteries.

Before entering the Great Pyramid, ancient initiates first needed to survive another test in one of the temples built for the left eye of Horus. One test required the initiate to take one breath of air before descending into a huge hole filled with water. Crocodiles lurked below, unknown to the student. Soon, thankfully, the student saw a light above the water and exited via the exit above. Having reached safety, however, the student would be told that he had taken the wrong exit and needed to repeat the test. Reentering the water, now known to have crocodiles, the student would have to dive deeper down to find the true exit. Surviving that sort of terror, one might be ready for the Great Pyramid.

Archeologists have found white crystalline powder in the king's chamber in the Great Pyramid. This powder has been thought to be pineal gland excretion left by initiates, or else a substance, manna, which is related to immortality. (See the chapter, Manna and the 21st Century). To become an immortal in full god-consciousness was the hope of former pharaohs. Today, it is known that pyramids preserve grains and fruits, and help germinate ancient seeds. Pyramid flowers are drier but maintain their intense color. Sliced dried apples still taste fresh and mummified raisins do not taste like raisins but like fresh grapes no matter how old they get. And pyramids remove the "fatigue" of materials and tools such as razors by realignment of crystalline edges.

The Great Pyramid is said to be a calendar marking historical periods via pyramid inches (each inch equals a year) and where passages and chambers meet or intersect. The calendar starts with the pyramid's construction, and proceeds to "mark" a timeline which includes the exodus of Moses, the birth of Jesus, the crucifixion of Christ, World War I, World War II, the atomic bomb in 1945, the discovery of DNA in 1953, and the appearance of the Hopi's Blue Star in 1987. Some researchers postulate that the pyramid predicts that in 2034 is the return of Christ, 2001 years after Calvary.

There is a rumor that the timeline approaches an end at the King's chamber on May 5, 2000. On that date, all the major planets will align—Mercury, Venus, Mars, Uranus, Neptune, on one side of the Sun, and Earth and Moon on the other side of the Sun. This alignment seems basically benign to both astronomers and astrologers, but the rumor is that this alignment will create eclipses and gravitational distortions and that the earth's crust may move in a polar shift, the last one being around 10,000 to 12,000 years ago, with floods, earthquakes, and global hurricanes of 1,000 m.p.h. Such cataclysmic change also occurred in the days of Noah and the Great Flood, and also perhaps coinciding with the end days of Atlantis. During the last polar shift, land movement was so abrupt that it interrupted peacefully feeding animals like the mammoths. A polar shift is not the same as continents drifting in opposite directions over millions of years. The future may hold a gradual polar shift, (a definite magnetic shift is under way) less a flip-flop, and more a slight turn. Presently, there is ice built up at the poles over two miles thick, a possible cause of wobble as the earth rotates. Antarctica sits in water that is as warm as the Mediterranean sea; glaciers are melting in Switzerland.

On the pyramid's time line the limestone floor in the antechamber ends and an Aswan granite floor composed of crystal quartz begins, which leads directly into the king's chamber. This change from limestone to crystal quartz stone begins February 21, 1999. This may mean that time ends as we know it—the end of linear time and the onset of seeing into the crystal multidimensional being.[6] (The Mayan calendar ends in 2012. A new cycle starts.)

The Great Pyramid may be the physical brain for the planet earth. But since we are ignorant of its uses and revelations, humanity may be missing an important initiation. And one may wonder, since pyramids following the Great Pyramid are inferior in construction, if human brain anatomy and function has also deteriorated from an earlier golden age? After the Great Pyramid was constructed, the ancient Egyptians were unable to duplicate it. They could copy the Great Pyramid externally but not the internal mathematical constants. Pyramids have been built all over the earth except Antarctica and Australia, with rumors of them even in Alaska. But compared to the construction of the Great Pyramid at Giza, all are of inferior design. Lost is the original knowledge with the original builders, whom some surmise were Atlanteans.

Within our own anatomy, from the base of the skull to the pineal gland, can be formed a triangle like the shape of the Great Pyramid. (One may see a picture of the Great Pyramid and the Eye of Horus on a one dollar bill.) Completing this pyramid are the descending pathways from the cerebral cortex to the spinal cord. These pathways reach the pyramidal and extra-pyramidal structures located in the medulla oblongata (the motor brain stem). The above echoes the ascending and descending passages of the Great Pyramid, from the Eye of Horus to the bottomless pit. If our own brain anatomy were initiated into a full conscious state, it could be Atlantis all over again.

In 1939, Edgar Cayce said in trance that about half of North Americans were Atlantean souls reincarnated. (Cayce stated that he remembered his own past life in Atlantis.) Atlantean technology was to be seen again in the twentieth century.

The body of the Egyptian Sphinx is deeply eroded by water, not wind or sand. If the Sphinx was once under water, was this the Great Flood of Noah? If there was water in the Sahara desert, this suggests that the Sphinx must be at least seven thousand to ten thousand years old (and likely far older, a relic of Atlantis), carved before the Egyptians arrived.

Edgar Cayce predicted in a trance that a chamber would be found in front of the Sphinx's paws and that it would contain records of the Atlantean race.[7] Seismography has indeed detected a rectangular cavity buried in front of the Sphinx's paws. Will the records be openly public, or will they be secreted away like the Marion seals? The burial of the Hall of Records beneath the front of the Egyptian Sphinx's paws was in the age of Leo—12,000 years ago. Some students of the mysteries say that the Hall of Records will be opened as soon as August 6, 1999 to 2005.

Gordon Michael Scallion began having prophetic earth visions in 1979, and then again in 1991. Educated in electronics, he worked in the field of communications. In 1977 he experienced a health crisis in which he lost his voice. In a hospital he saw a light and a woman/angel who spoke of what would happen in his lifetime. She called this period of history "the time of choosing" and referred to it as the "tribulation." Scallion then had a series of twenty-nine nightmares, and visions that foretold of an increased frequency of earth changes, including the breakup of the United States, beginning mostly in 1992 and intensifying afterward. (He has in distribution, The Future Map of the United States: 1998-2012.) Overall, the changes on this map are to be taken as high probability, but not absolute. He has predicted many violent earth changes accurately, including the Los Angeles earthquakes of April 22, 1991 and June 28, 1991 and their magnitudes of 6.0 and 7.0 on the Richter scale (although magnitudes are reported lower at times for insurance and disaster money savings). According to Scallion, most of the early earth changes have already occurred: Hurricane Andrew, the two quakes in California of 1992, and the July 12, 1993 quake in Japan. More quakes of huge magnitude are to come, and enormous activity in the dynamics between the North American plate and the Pacific plate. As the North American tectonic plate pushes against the Pacific plate, low level infrasound will be detected by some people, and related flu-like symptoms will result as the inner ear is affected. The hum will be heard mostly in New Mexico, Nevada, Arizona and California. The Taos hum in northern New Mexico is well publicized. No one has been able to explain it.

According to Scallion, the first great warning is when Mount Rainier in Washington State erupts. Ash falls in Seattle. (In 1994, Awareness Warnings were being issued in Washington State due to activity detected in the core of Mount Rainier.) A third quake with a magnitude over 8.5 on the Richter scale will occur in Los Angeles. These former events signal the breakup of the United States.

After the early changes, a quake of over 9 magnitude erupts in Mexico City and people flood northward. Supermega quakes of 10 to 15 on the Richter scale also hit Bakersfield, Eureka, San Diego and Sonoma County. A first fracture in the West will start from Eureka, California and extend through Bakersfield to Baja, California. There will be a new temporary coast, and water rushes in. California becomes the Isles of California.

On the California-Nevada border, there will be the birth of a new volcano. Then, the second West Coast fracture will occur along another unknown fault line from Newport Oregon to Phoenix, Arizona. The North American plate cracks under pressure against the Pacific plate and slides down. Thus, much of the western states will be under water, the new coast wending from Phoenix, Arizona to Denver to Norfolk, Nebraska. Scallion 'saw' vessels coming into these ports in a vision. Migrations east follow; Californians set up tent cities, many in Colorado and New Mexico. Meanwhile, the Great Lakes spill and divide the continent, with a new waterway between Illinois and Indiana down to the Gulf and coast of Texas, flooding most of Louisiana. A bridge will be built to connect the two smaller continents of the United States. The East Coast also has earthquakes beginning in New York. The Manhattan inland waterway loses thirty percent of its land. Florida loses fifty percent of its land. Hawaii will have one less island and Alaska will be greatly inundated.

After the purification, Scallion's visions are of an increased telepathy in humans—a lunar society guided by intuition. Healing occurs; sound and color therapies become the new approach. New flowers, clean air. Long cigar-shaped craft glide silently over ground without wheels. The average lifespan becomes 150 years. The plagues of the tribulation are gone. The children now become the root race parents of the children of the Blue Ray. Scallion foresees that Earth will have a binary star system. The second sun will appear during day hours as a small white light in sky, similar to the moon when it is visible during day hours. In the evening, this sun will appear 10 times the size and brightness of other stars. Because of this second sun, all races on earth will have a blue cast to their skin.

Scallion's visions include the collapse of the United States government and the creation of "The New Thirteen Colonies." Each colony will represent one of the lunar months. There will be sacred sites to reaffirm spirituality, these being located at the Island at Mount Shasta, Sedona, Arizona, the Green Mountains of Vermont and the Serpent Mound of Ohio. The Shawnees at Serpent Mound are presently working to become sovereign, and to reestablish a spiritual center.

While much land will flood, other land will rise. Atlantis will rise, the ruins of its great cities to be found in the Bahamas, Azores, Gulf of Mexico and Sargasso Sea. Power domes will be found that use solar energy and are active after 12,000 years. In the Pacific Ocean, Mu, the ancient City of Gold and capital of Lemuria, will rise after 54,000 years. Its ancient records will be understood by the new Blue Ray, children who will psychically read the holographic messages in the sculptures that will be found.

As noted in the 1997 issue 17 of *Ancient American* magazine, a well preserved ancient city was found in the spring of 1995 in the waters of southern Japan off Okinawa. The structures do not show effects of cataclysm despite Japan's history of frequent earthquakes. These structures had instead been gradually inundated with water. The last time the sea waters were as low as twenty-five meters (the depth at which the Yonaguni pyramidal platform was found) was at least 7,000 to 8,000 years ago. Most oceanographers insist the seas were down twenty-five meters 1 to 1.7 million years ago (about 500,000 years before the presumed evolution of man). The Japanese are quite open to the idea and the notion of Mu (Lemuria is the Roman name) existing at an ancient time. In northern Japan is a river named Mu.

On June 9, 1994, a quake of 8.6 magnitude which struck 338 to 395 miles beneath La Paz, Bolivia shook Toronto, Canada. This is the deepest quake ever recorded, and there is no scientific explanation at present to explain how a quake could originate so deep inside the Earth. Edgar Cayce forecasted an earthquake which would shake a continent from one end to another. Such a frightful prediction would have suggested untold annihilation at the surface. But we all survived since the quake was so deep. Though it shook two continents, only the seismograph needles moved. He also predicted that in the 1970's the East Coast would be completely deluged under water. What happened was Watergate. At the level of psyche—the truest reality—his prediction did manifest. A great flood may be a physical event that takes place in the heavens. Astrologers point out that there is a swallowing up, or flooding/drowning, of star groups as a result of the cyclical processional motion of the planet earth.

Weather changes have always wreaked havoc. In 1556, 830,000 people in China died in a quake. In 1755 in Lisbon, 60,000 people died in a quake. In 1923 a quake killed over 140,000 people in Tokyo and Yokohama.

In the spring 1994 newsletter, *The Total Perspective*, R. E. McMaster Jr., a very successful and intuitive businessman, says climate is the great ignored economic factor. He foresees the end to oil companies and many present corporations. He looks at investment in environmental cleanup prospects. He says to invest in technologies that will soon replace public utilities and oil. He notes that precious metals and magnets will be used to cure cancer, and that a new technique will convert water into a fire that destroys toxic wastes. He writes of a battery with a useful life of 40,000 years and of a true perpetual motion machine. He says to buy organic farming land. He is practical and visionary, and reflects what the new businessman will be.

We are given the minerals of Earth and the visions of heaven, but we still need a human-sized relationship to the Earth. We are reminded to stay close to earth by the tiny chalky stones called otoliths that are inside the chamber of one's ear. Otoliths fall downwards toward the earth, the pressure of the stones sending signals to the brain that say, "this way is down." This way is earth. God is in your neighbor made of clay, perhaps Heaven in the physical, an experience of Reath. But spirit is where the temple is lighted within.

In the book of Revelation, the new city of Jerusalem has no temple, for God is there. There is no more moon or sun, for the dualities of energy vanish, and all is lighted from within:

"I saw no temple therein: for the lord God Almighty and the Lamb are the temple of it. And the city had no need of the sun, neither of the moon, to shine in it: for the glory of God did lighten it, and the Lamb is the light thereof."

Revelation (21:22)

LOVE NOTES OF A STUDENT
BEFORE ERASING

Let's go away, You and I;
I am restless
in this tight-bricked classroom.
I doodle Picasso elephants

Let's go away,
try Stonehenge by moonlight,
go telepathic,
or go down under to Ayer's Rock
so huge it creates its own weather.

Let's go,
our hearts
impala and bird.
Africa at midday
sudden turn of the rhino's horn.

Let's you and I
meet in the zoo this night.
I am restless, telepathic, and huge.
The moon that enters the cages
becomes the African moon.

Notes:

—Ayer's Rock, located in central Australia, is a reddish sandstone which can be seen 60 miles away. It is 1,143 feet tall with a girth almost six miles and it creates its own weather.

—The earth's magnetic field is collapsing—the magnetic flow from the iron core is less, and the wobble is more, with a build-up of ice at the poles.

—Carl Jung wrote that whatever is not accepted as part of the Self appears in the outer world as an event. Emotion and coherent thought play a part in earth changes, and some say in quantum physics and sacred geometry. Prophets say this.

—Edgar Cayce in trance said that the great Pyramid was built after the fall of Atlantis. Building began in 10,490 B.C. and required a century. Many have postulated that sound helped move the stones.

—Pluto entered Sagittarius in November 1995, and will remain there for the next thirteen years. Historically, when Pluto has entered Sagittarius, the world has seen Jesus, Pericles, Charlemagne, Luther, The Golden Age of Greece (465), The High Renaissance of Italy (1501-1516), the Inquisition and the Enlightenment, Mozart; the Stamp Act that led to the American Revolution. During the coming period of Pluto in Sagittarius, hyper-religiosity will erupt along with the true higher spirit. Institutions will break apart. There will be a flourishing of social tribalism and gated communities versus corporate downsizing. An increase in cottage industries, and more private schools. American know-how will reemerge. (The twentieth century was a renaissance of technology, music, and psychology.)

—The Great Purification of Earth and humanity is a promise of spiritual awakening and is not to be equated with the horrors of ethnic/racial "cleansing."

Chapter 12

The Dream Mind

"Behold, this dreamer cometh."

–Genesis (37:19)

"No live organism can continue for long to exist sanely under conditions of absolute reality. Even larks and katydids are supposed by some to dream."

–Shirley Jackson

Dreams have been called the language of God. My husband dreamt of an Englishman who was troubled because science had left out God. The Englishman then went off somewhere to think. Meanwhile, having given up the science of his day, he began to experience the proof of God in everyday life. Church bells behind him rang louder and louder. Carl Jung viewed the unconscious, its symbols and dreams, as if "God had passed over some of his power and responsibility to one."[1] The American inventor Isaac Singer (1811-1875), struggling to find the correct needle design for a practical home sewing machine, dreamt of African natives who wielded spears saying they would eat him if he didn't invent it. Then he noticed a spear which was actually the type of needle shape he wanted.

I had a dream wherein I was working in a critical cardiac care unit. The EKG strips did not show the usual lined electrical patterns for the heart, but instead were cubist paintings. I thought, the heart, Picasso's "Girl with a Mandolin".

The measure of time is different in dreams from waking. Dial clocks in dreams keep fairly accurate time, the hands moving in a circle, while digital clocks in dreams are unreliable—any number pops up.[2] Dream time is in wholes versus digital bits. Dream time is a view without an ego. It is a face whose dial sweeps round, gathering hours into seasons, the hours almost touch like the dreams my dreams have.

Dreams have neither definite beginnings nor endings, going back through past lives to the beginning of time, even to the mind that dreamed this universe into being. We may sometimes pick up on the future dream. In *Mass Dreams of the Future*, a group of subjects in the 1980s were hypnotically progressed into the future to the year 2050. These subjects reported that human eye color had changed, that the iris was a "deep violet."[3] Humanity at that time is sensing something in the skies, specifically the presence of "Christ-consciousness." An event related to this time was of a bright light in the sky moving at a tremendous rate of speed but in complete silence. When the object landed, it was an aircraft in the shape of a spaceship. The occupants emerged wearing silver jumpsuits and indicated that they had come to help clean up the planet of dangerous radioactivity which was liberated during an earlier "shift." They greeted the earthlings, saying, "Welcome to the human race."[4]

At seven months the human fetus dreams, has REM. It dreams in the womb, yet there is no light in the womb. The poet Blake wrote: "Another Sun feeds our life streams." Where does the light and imagery in dreams come from? Dreams have been described as internal holograms projected from the mind. (Holograms are images produced by a split beam of laser light.) There are two types of holographic images, virtual and real. The virtual image of a hologram has no more extension in space than does an image in a mirror. One may look into it and learn. Then it may cease to be. The "real image" does have extension in space, and is not illusion. Dreams are projections into virtual and real space. Dreams are internal holograms.[5] Holograms can be shattered, but in each piece is still a picture of the whole. The actor Christopher Reeves, who fell off a horse and became paralyzed in the summer of 1995, says that at night in his dreams he is still riding horses and is "whole."

A woman told me of a dream in which she was "a Frenchman stalling German soldiers" who had approached the house where she was hiding war refugees. But then, a soldier noticed a movement in the window of a cellar-like room in the house, and she/the Frenchman was shot. A girl hidden in the house ran to the woods and escaped. The woman's daughter had the same dream, only she was the girl in the house who escaped to the woods. Both mother and daughter question if this was a past life memory.

I remember a child patient I cared for at a state hospital. She was only a figment of the physical world.

THE VISIT: STATE HOSPITAL

Tubes. Hunger only ghosts now;
the harmony of my hands look intimately elsewhere.
Drawer of letters. Cut stems.
We both fall apart in this reckless creation.
Here, a blanket around you.
a doll for your heart to woo
in some sad interlude
when your arms should not lay forgotten

Should I tell you
of the roaming I will have to do
across this floor
how no one will answer why
you are less than these tiles?

But I will answer
because you are a dream
that becomes invertebrate
except that I am here
and remember you.

Most real is the mind itself, where its projections are its manifestation, or perhaps its camouflage. Seth, the channel of Jane Roberts, says that the inner senses "do Not parallel the outer senses because there is nothing to be seen, heard or touched in the manner in which you are accustomed." (However, Carl Jung noticed that Europeans emigrating to the United States would begin to have American and native American motifs in their dreams, that the soil one touches affects dream life. What dreams will unfold as astronauts visit the Moon, Mars, or simply deep space?) From the inner mind come fragments, or egos which identify with the outer world and camouflage themselves with it. But what is ultimately wanted is what the poet Antonio Machado wrote: "What the poet is searching for is not the fundamental I, but the deep You."

INTERIOR POSE

Some water nudges it
this desert where often I stare
inaudible at the window

I see stones where there is nothing
ask what loneliness placed them there.

From the table I can see her
brushing her hair. I lament.

What mirror is our interior pose,
what wind moves in a mirror?

Wind is the discontent of caves
calling deeper to find itself
find what is in this window's understanding

Lucid dreaming is the ability to be awake and aware in your dreams, to see from the inner eye of the whole self. Lucid dreams have a clarity and exhilaration related to being in a world free of waking time and space. One can joyfully experiment with the projections of the mind, while realizing one is dreaming. One may alter the contents of the dream by mental will. Because gravity is absent in dreams, one can fly and whisk through ceilings. One may be aware of being in two places at once. In lucid dreaming, the dream-world and out-of-body "death" state intersect at least. The excursions out are less "out of body" than "into the mind." One experiences space-time behind physical reality. There is no biological explanation for lucid dreaming. Though there is no death in dreams, only transformations of energy, we respect the "illusion" of three-dimensional time and space. That is, we don't sit on railroad tracks flirting with trains, because the earthly ego would naturally be run over.

A recent technology, a dream-light, enables users to lucid dream more easily, as the goggles sense when the dreamer is in REM and then flashes a red light that is enough to be recognized in the dream-state, but not so intense as to awaken the person. However, "Eighty percent of the time the light takes on aspects of the dream world, seamlessly woven into the dream," so one must learn to recognize the light when the signal comes.[6] An example is given in Stephen Laberge's book, *Exploring the World of Lucid Dreaming*:

> On a trip—we are descending a mountain. Twice covering my whole field of vision, I see glorious brilliant patterns in red, radiating from a central point. I call them "Sufi fireworks" and think they must have been produced to prevent us from seeing something. I feel I know something about the significance of this journey that my companions do not.[7]

The above lucid experience suggests that the ego that falls asleep cannot be the exact one that wakes up in the dream.

Tibetans are among the cultures wherein lucid dreaming is considered ultimately to be the way humans dream—or else we are dreaming like animals. Cultures that lucid dream have been credited with superior mental and physical health. To not know the dream-body and the dream-mind, it is as if the whole of us is an energy or consciousness wasted.

> She thinks,
> why be a mindless apple
> that simply falls?

A Malaysian tribe, the Senoi, believes dreams can be dealt with consciously inside oneself so that a conflict need not happen outside. If one kills a lion, or enemy, first in a dream, then one will have obviated the need to do so in waking. Henry III of France, after dreaming that the animals in his menagerie were planning to eat him, personally killed them all, on January 20, 1583.[8] He acted out his dream as fate and not insight:

> You enter each cage
> rooster, monkey.

A dream that becomes "fate" may be interpreted as prescient. The dream thus predicts a coming outer phenomena. A woman once told me of a dream she had of her friend's mother which was of "an explosion, followed by a scene of a fawn eating eucalyptus leaves. I knew it had to do with my friend's mother. Two weeks later the mother died of a stroke. I knew she was deeply at peace on the other side."

In the early 1950's it was discovered that we dream—at least the Western scientific community credited itself with the discovery of an electrical phenomenon called REM, or Rapid Eye Movement. In the 1950's it was thought by scientists that sleep is for rest. Volumes have been learned since. Sleep has different stages:

> Stage I: relaxation—in order to transition into sleep. A bridge between wakefulness and true sleep. A person may appear to be sleeping, but be electrically awake.
> Stage II: restores autonomic nervous system, body rhythms, clocks, temperature, heart rate, respiration. The clocks of the brain are related to circadean cycles. The largest portion of the night is spent in this stage.
> Stage III & IV: deep sleep that restores tissue via protein synthesis, and growth hormone released from the pituitary.
> REM (dreaming): restores memory and mood. REM follows each cycle—becoming longer as night continues. New findings show that we dream also outside of REM. Seth says REM is the electrical

activity which occurs after the soul comes back into the body. (In sleep, the aura expands outwardly two inches from the body; during REM, the aura jumps out thirteen feet.)

All sleep is restorative. Stage IV or deep sleep, so prominent in youth, may be the Fountain of Youth. After the age of twenty or so, there are lesser amounts of stage IV sleep. Sleep stages and architecture change as one matures. Infants have REM and deep sleep only, for the most part. Between the ages of sixty and eighty, one gets less deep sleep and less REM. From age eighty-five into the nineties, sleep patterns change again.

The Hindu Upanishads speak of four states of sleep. First is ordinary wakefulness. The second is a subtle composure of light. The third is deep sleep that is unified, composed of bliss, and the fourth state is "the source of all, both the origin and the end of contingent beings." The fourth is enlightenment where one never really goes to sleep at all—the Brahman Self that is lucid at all times in its great dream.

On the television show "Unsolved Mysteries," in May 1993, a psychic named George Anderson was studied by a New York sleep lab. He was found to have very unusual sleep patterns. He has only one hemisphere of his brain asleep at a time.[9] Dolphins and whales have one hemisphere always "awake" while the other hemisphere dreams/sleeps. Thus they don't drown, and part of them is always dreaming.

In her book, *Life Before Life*, Helen Wambach, Ph.D. hypnotically regressed an identical twin who recalled a past life with his other twin half. In utero they felt telepathic with each other, and they had also been together in the between-life state. Thus, both decided to reincarnate as twins. But then the one twin died. When the other felt him receding from the fetus, he said he knew the twin brother would "come to me in my dreams in this life."[10]

DREAM WOMB

A night ferry shimmers
like the Big Dipper

its wheel turns stars
into water

a steward says,
"It is time."
and you climb the ramp

blue-violet wavelets splash
the ferry's hull

wheel turns river to dream

Notes:

—Sometimes it is revealing to view waking life as a dream; events that would otherwise appear meaningless, or disruptive and from without, can then approach oneself as a symbol and an act. The great play that one is a part of will become more clear, and a true dialogue with the world ensues.

Preface To Psychedelia

The French Revolution was partly fueled by caffeine. Caffeine was thought to be mentally stimulating and even hallucinogenic. At the height of a cappuccino addiction, I had a dream of a marble goddess, twenty-two feet high, who sprang from my espresso machine.

CAPPUCCINO GODDESS

A white steam, and a white goddess
the woman says amused, I do love my Cappuccino
and several cups conjure you
the goddess answers, her voice kind
it is magic to you now, so do not abuse
the woman answers, I do prefer this cup
over anything
the goddess says, you are obsessed
for now be blessed
and the woman gives thanks to the goddess
asks, should she
sprinkle nutmeg, or cinnamon
on her cappuccino?

Chapter 13

Psychedelia And The Light Brain

"How can the eyes see the sun unless they are sunlike themselves?"

–Goethe

No eye ever saw the sun without becoming sunlike."

–Plotinus, Enneads (1.6.9)

Psychedelics are substances derived from plants. Plants, in general, are said to have more primary perception, or a nature closer to what is behind all of nature. Having no nervous system, no organs to "see" or "hear" with, the plant experiences the world without the fragmentation of the five senses.

Plant timing is slower than ours. The early twentieth century Viennese biologist Raoul Francé suggested that plants move their bodies as freely as humans do, but that they do so at a much slower pace.[1] The slower pace of plants is like a contemplation, or a being-ness. Blossoms dream their falls onto the shady-bricked streets.

In Latin, "hallucinari" means "to wander in the mind." What could be more human? A man was given LSD in a therapy session.

He "saw" a rose in his hand. When his thoughts said, "forget all this and drink," the rose withered. When he thought of staying sober, the rose bloomed. The man said, "the LSD allowed me to see my own mind." He has been sober ever since. His wife says, "He is a peaceful man at last. He would be dead of alcoholism if not for the LSD."

Psychedelics (delos means "clear" and psyche relates to mind, in Greek) are related to natural compounds like serotonin which are within our normal brain chemistry. Serotonin is related to a class of indole alkaloids which includes psychedelics like LSD-25 and the psilocybin of some mushrooms. Serotonin enhances the creation of light within the brain when transduced to melatonin, a molecule that changes chemical energy to light. From within the brain, light is created. This may be related to the light in dreams. Or light created from dark—from the Big Bang came the million suns, and from mushrooms growing in dung, we ingest a light. Both the brain and heart are saturated with melanin molecules. The enlightened state includes both heart and mind. Serotonin abounds in bananas and plums, and in figs, especially the *Ficus religiosa*, known in India as the Bo-tree, under which the Buddha reportedly sat when he became enlightened. Psilocybin mushrooms have been associated with human brain chemistry since ancient times. The use of these psychedelics goes back to humanity's origins in Africa. Terence McKenna, author of *Food of the Gods*, writes that psilocybin mushrooms complete, in a symbiotic manner, the human nervous system, bringing to it the human qualities of self-consciousness, reflectiveness, imagination, sense of community, and increased visual acuity.[2] One associates shamanism and vision quests with hallucinogenics. Terence McKenna purports that early humankind's relationship with mushrooms accounts for the sudden growth spurt of the neocortex or light brain during the end of the last Ice Age.

Serotonin may be an "older" neurotransmitter; whereas the bonding of harmine into the genetic material of the cerebral neurons/DNA "could form permanent bonds maintained by a form of superconductivity" writes Terence and Dennis McKenna in *The Invisible Landscape*. Harmine, a "resonant transmitter" of the informational hologram stored in DNA, is the ticket to long-term memory storage. Even "conceiving an idea would create a specific wave form pattern of tryptamine-RNA resonation, where this resonated sympathetically on the superconducting DNA-harmine macromolecule, that part of the molecular chain would be held holographically as a three-dimensional image."[3] DNA is thus more than a sequential readout, in that every cell has identical nucleotide sequences that can regenerate the entire organism. (It is due to the presence of certain inductors, notably RNA, that DNA makes some cells into skin, others into neurons, muscle, etc.)

In India, the cow may have earned its status as sacred because in ancient times, out of its dung sprung the hallucinogenic mushroom *Stropharia cubensis*. Presently, however, there is not any *Stropharia cubensis*, nor the plant, Soma, in India. *Stropharia cubensis* is still on the planet. The Soma plant's botanical identity remains a mystery, and is debatable, but was praised in the sacred Rig Veda.

A Floridian took mushrooms from old cow dung, and then sunshine was even transfigured, muck of tadpoles, frogs, ponds, arose in swampy earth patterns. No birds were seen.

Joseph Campbell said in an interview "the supernatural life is the bouquet of nature, not something imposed upon it." Abstract cerebrations alone cannot substitute for the organic perceptual experience. Throughout the Bible, angels give prophets rolls to eat. (Note that the prophets eat the roll, they don't smoke or inject it.) It is sad to see moderns praying to an empty host, but what happens in the heart is the most primary gift; it simply happens more fully with real substance conductors. Thus, modern brains isolated from spiritual foods, or the mushroom, are incomplete at the chemical synapse level. Not having hallucinogens is like not having a kind of chemistry of love. Those without such an initiation view those on psychedelics to be as silly as people "in love."

The brain is a sensual organ, and Mother Nature is hallucinatory, a cupboard of wild beauty.

The mycelia of mushrooms is a complex network that our own brains hook into—like an organic Internet. The mycelia are nearly immortal, like a god. The spores can survive space travel, and possibly have over millennia. They land on psyche like landing on the moon. The mycelium of mushrooms can cover several acres— bluff of river feeds what is unseen.

Mrs. Gelpke, a graphic artist, had never been to Mexico. While in Switzerland, she ingested Mexican mushrooms and began to draw elaborate Mexican designs. A few months later she did travel to Mexico and was amazed by the similarities of her drawings with

Mexican designs. Albert Hofmann also ingested the Mexican mushroom, *Psilocybin mexicana*, in Switzerland in the mid-fifties, and he was "overwhelmed by Mexican imagery despite attempts to focus on other things."[4]

Psychedelic connections are also vast conceptually. Aldous Huxley wrote of his own experience on mescaline when, "Words like 'grace' and 'transfiguration' came to my mind."[5] The delightful and the beautiful are the heavens of psychedelics, but also there are encounters that are hellish. Jean-Paul Sartre chose to be injected in 1935 with mescaline and he experienced being pursued by giant lobsters thereafter. His existential novel, *Nausea* (1938), was derived from this nightmare.

Dr. Stanislov Grof has rebirthed many subjects on LSD, and the results have been compared to transformations that have come about in ancient temple mysteries and rites. Archetypes like the Great Mother, paradise, hell, purgatory, historical scenes, complex mandalas, past and future lives, episodes in the birth womb, have all been encountered. Visions of blinding light, death-rebirth rites, resurrection, and journeys out-of-body have all been experienced. Paintings depicting these can be found in Grof's book, *Beyond the Brain: Birth, Death, and Transcendence in Psychotherapy*.

LSD is a very potent psychedelic derived from the laboratory and so has minimal history with humankind compared to mushrooms. Yet, it may be what the philosopher Gerald Heard thought—a gift of consciousness given by God to us in the twentieth century, a device to save humanity from Armageddon. The use of LSD and other psychedelic brain foods in the 1960's rock era altered perceptions forever. The 1960's youth movement has been compared to the Christians dropping out of Rome.

HAIGHT-ASHBURY FLOWER

a young woman stands on the Haight
homeless pollen is all her bad habits

but like the others in the park
she is full of hope

and she lies down
in the titanic spaces of grass

in a dark green shade
the scent of its deep
is her skin

this is home
this is peace

In the 1990s, hemp may well spawn a revolution. The Green Party has candidates endorsing its legality. Hemp is a 100 percent biodegradable, nontoxic and non-polluting plant. Its fibers can be woven for durable clothing, rope and twine. It saves trees. Soon, the grocery sacker will ask, "Paper, plastic, or hemp?" Hemp seed oil is usable for paints and varnishes, has medicinal properties and its essential fatty acids are exceptionally well configured for humans. Hemp seed oil without THC (the psychoactive ingredient in marijuana) even liquefies saturated fats, and mobilizes hydrogenated, refined fat out. (Ingestion of THC is natural, versus smoking which is linked to problems with driving safely, infertility, amotivational syndrome, and lung cancer.)

The Hmong, emigrating from Cambodia and Vietnam, were not allowed by the U.S. government to keep their hemp seeds which they use for clothing, paper, oils, etc. Ironically, the first two drafts of the Declaration of Independence were written on hemp paper. (Hemp paper can last for centuries.) Hemp seeds are found at virtually all archeological sites.

Recreational use of psychedelics is very strongly discouraged by this author. Certain meditation practices can bring about similar effects and insights in an integrative way, unlocking internal natural chemistry. It is a loss that there are not teachers in the mainstream United States culture to guide a spiritual rite with use of sacred foods.

THE ROCKLAMB
(for Janis Joplin, who died of alcohol and heroin abuse)

(In bygone days it could be the loss of Mozart to alcohol,
or Freud to cocaine, or Miles Davis to heroin. In the
romantic age, the poets Shelley and Coleridge experimented with hashish and opium, respectively.)

Little Lamb, you are a lamb.
I am a hungry, lonely lamb.
What prey for a wolf
crouched in fleece?
In the Judas Song
in a wail song.
You are clever for a lamb.
I hear wolf packs running in your head.

God is Dead Flower children
suck the Rocklamb like wild roots
clinging, filling in,
smacking salty rain there, Sing!

Rich hippie at the Woodstock frolic
how do rock gardens grow?
Granite scraped inside out.
gravel gouged out the gut.

Do rocks grow old?
They sing to dust.
Stardom blows the rest into cold
wax like weighted light.

In a blackhole
the rocklamb thought
it was the flowers that prettied it.

The danger in recreational use and massive doses of a
hallucinogenic like LSD-25 (or more accurately, an amplifier of
reality) lies in that the substance chemically activates all levels of

cellular memory. A kind of psychosis (the word psychosis meaning, "an intoxication of the psyche") is induced. Then cellular memory may emerge unpredictably, so that one's ego (your physical image in relation to the outer world) is not in the forefront anymore. The ego, of course, cannot be annihilated. Destroy one and another takes over, though more fragile. The Self doesn't easily run out of egos. Since we are part of nature and its inner vitality, when one steps outside of a familiar ego, another source of ourselves and nature is revealed and encountered, and new alliances occur with the Self. This can be a positive rebirth if experienced in a protective setting. The usual problem for humans, however, is that we have an ego that needs to shake itself loose now and then, but doesn't do so because that feels like death. Aldous Huxley, author of *The Doors Of Perception*, while dying, chose to enhance the experience by being on LSD. The LSD did not cause his death, of course.

* * * * * * *

The man and woman entered the woods in August, to ensure plenty of light for the long trip. She ate half a paper. The forest was already beautiful, grassy as two Aprils. They wore dark sunglasses as their eyes would dilate in wonder and sensitivity. She whispered to the man, "Let's try to keep a low profile." The path had pines up the slope to the right, and the creek gorge was to the left. With summer sun above, they found a place to settle out of sight, under a group of trees the shade of a peacock feather. The man said, "Maybe it isn't working. Maybe it isn't what they say it is." By that time she already had a cosmic giggle, her voice like butterflies that walk along a ridge. "I know, it's working for you," he retorted, "I probably have a more rigid ego—maybe I should eat the other half." But then the motor of the universe turned off, quiet as a plant. Their bodies, slowed, were actually feeling electric, stepped up—cells of light and mind. He could see into bark. She whispered, "Don't move, because that will rearrange everything." Time disappeared, a watch, a superfluous gadget strewn in the pine needles. Space was everywhere and nowhere. She began to measure the forest—not by rulers, but by meaning perceived in the center. For a few moments they spoke to each other telepathically, and he sent his thoughts through the ethers to her. They instantly grasped what the sacred Vedas teach. Here there is no death. She felt a profound innocence that today she associates with the notion of the Lamb of the World. They were in the mysteries and even imagined mass resurrections. He commented, "This is incredible. No amount of meditation can do this. The Yogis, they must have cheated." They saw all the suns of the world—a polar sun and a tropical sun. A vast reflective aliveness was in all things. The intelligent crow, its voice deep, swished over, ushered in something in the solar plexus. My god, the crow is more intelligent than we! Then the trees and clouds began to stiffen again, and they started down the hill. A few humans on the trail they walked by were a bit ghoulish, vociferous, zombie-like except for tiny beacons somewhere in their skulls. An Audubon group approached with binoculars. That sent a fright. The idea of making small talk seemed absurd, even impossible to deliver at this level. But then the Audubon group walked away through some brush like a herd of deer.

* * * * * *

Psychedelics are not all alike. Lab synthesized LSD-25 has characteristics quite different from nature-picked psilocybin mushrooms. Below is a comparison between the two:

LSD:
Electric. Whitman's "I Sing the Body Electric"
Fractals everywhere, see into clouds, into bark
verbal expression difficult
ecstasy, psychosis dis-connected state
are somewhere high off the planet
so much light must wear sunglasses
center of universe is everywhere
resurrections easily imagined
the Father in Heaven

PSILOCYBIN Mushroom:
Magnetic
softer organic light, almost webbed
the most complex visuals, colors—rich blue peacocks
ultimate imagination, infinite nesting as in the chaos
    term
can talk about experience
memory intact, more body experience

must cover eyes to see inner light—like a mushroom
ancient scenery, Mu, "Now I am back with the blue
  monkeys."
reincarnation mysteries
early jungles and ancient rites/initiations
direct connection with Mother Earth consciousness

Psychedelics provide portals for experience to give us what we need. A woman ate a half paper of LSD and the experience was of an anvil, an ongoing apocalypse of each new ego as it arose—a rhythmic climb to the god Logos. She saw many levels of heavens. Months later, eating the other half paper, the enigmatic, charming Sophia called "I'm here, no here," in soft touches, more capriciously. Her mind was whole as the paper was whole.

Notes:

—The melanin molecule is reduced from melatonin (a human chlorophyll which holds/tranduces light). Melanin is a light molecule that saturates the heart and brain. It creates light inside the brain and heart, wherein the photons are chemically translated. An energy wave, even sound, can be pumped through the melanin molecule, and light waves result. Note that hallucinogens, such as LSD, can create the experience of hearing colors. The melanin protein complex crystal is related to light, even hindrance of light when it interferes with the monopoles that are present in the cell's mitochondria. The monopoles, or Caduccean coils receive light in the form of electromagnetic fields which convert to informational fields. That can be experienced at the level of the mental body. The mitochondria are where atomic reactions take place. Mitochondria are "alien" in that they were once separate, and then symbiotically connected up with our cells. All crystals in the human body are melanin protein complexes.
   —The heart has the intelligence of light as well as the brain. The heart is the first organ to develop.
   —Melatonin, possibly a youth elixir, drops greatly after puberty. This is when sexual reproduction becomes possible because death actually begins at the physiological level—the mythic idea of a "death hormone" began here, as growth hormone also drops. The

species is ready to replace itself. Melatonin should not be taken if there is a history of gonadal cancer. Melatonin is taken from the pineal gland of pig fetuses. It is helpful for those who have wake and sleep disturbances, or those with jet lag. Dreams are more vivid with higher melatonin levels. When light photons enter the pupil, the pineal gland is stimulated; the melatonin is produced at night. Adolescents become interested in death concepts, even if personally they feel immortal. Is this due to melatonin hormonal levels?

—From 1965 to 1967, a movement began in an old Victorian neighborhood in San Francisco, named Haight-Ashbury. Music exploded, as well as ingenious dress; poetry and articles like "Yoga and the Psychedelic Mind" and "The Imagination and the Delightful," and philosophy classes prospered. Ideas as large and generous as peace, love, harmony, and bliss flourished. Acupuncture, homeopathic medicine, eastern meditation and Indian music were rediscovered. Berkeley type politicos marched on Washington, D.C. to end the Vietnam War, while the hippies and Jesus freaks opted to drop out of society in order to tune in to ecstasy. The two met in the "Summer of Love" in 1967 at Golden State Park. The Be-in was a way that music and dance could heal the world and finally end the War. One hundred thousand pilgrims joined the Be-in.

—In Germany, alcoholism has been treated with LSD. This has been documented to be far more successful, in even a single session, than conventional treatments and even Alcoholics Anonymous, where two out of three people continue to relapse. LSD may cause chromosome breaks in the blood cells of LSD users, but these effects are neither long lasting or a cause of birth defects. However, reread the section on holographic DNA as viewed by the McKennas.

—In A.D. 994, an ergot toxicity outbreak from infected grain killed 40,000 people in France. Ergot toxicity produces delirium and gangrene. There is almost no toxicity to psilocybin mushrooms.

—Five hundred thousand youth were at Woodstock; there was virtually no theft and no crime despite use of pot, LSD, mushrooms and beer.

—The majority of violent crime and theft can be related to cocaine and to alcohol—one illegal, one legal. Psychedelic users rarely rob banks or commit violence. Selling LSD is not for money or power (it costs but a few dollars) but is for the mystical, the delightful. Tragically, a young man, age nineteen, was put in prison for ten years without parole for selling LSD. The U.S. army, in the 1950's and 60's, gave LSD to unsuspecting soldiers at the Edgewood Arsenal north of Baltimore, Maryland. This was probably a way to test mind control techniques, but instead they had men who walked in crooked lines, much as spiders who have taken LSD weave bizarre space time webs. The U.S. army did not sell or "push" (a propagandist term) LSD. They gave it to unaware soldiers. Where are their prison sentences? (Lethal chemicals and mustard gas were also given.)

—Albert Hofmann, former research chemist at Sandoz Pharmaceutical Company in Basel, Switzerland, accidentally discovered LSD-25 (lysergic acid diethylamide) when he absorbed it on his skin and tripped. He was studying alkaloids of ergot, a parasitic grain fungus, or rust.

—George Washington's diary includes his separating of the seeds of female and male hemp before the female was fertilized, which produces a potent seedless type of marijuana. While living in Mount Vernon, on Aug. 7, 1765, he wrote in his diary: "began to separate the male from the female hemp—rather too late" The reason to separate in midsummer before the females are fertilized is to produce a potent and rich resin seedless type of marijuana for "medicinal purposes."

—Tibetan Buddhists have extraordinarily complex mandala designs but are not usually users of hallucinogenics. Grof has had success using only breathing and music.

—LSD mimics the brain's internal neurotransmitters; "flashbacks" may mimic postraumatic stress syndrome.

—It is more dangerous for young people to use hallucinogenics than mature adults because in youth the brain is still organizing. Addiction, versus a rite of passage, constricts reality and the person becomes concrete in perception, not mind expanded.

—Three hundred thousand citizens are jailed for possession of marijuana each year (without having caused bodily harm), and ten billion dollars a year is spent on drug enforcement.

—The processing of hemp paper is far less polluting than processing pulp paper, wherein bleaching pulp paper with chlorine produces dioxin which is extremely poisonous and is also flushed into waterways.

—Ibogaine, a hallucinogenic plant found in western Africa, has been shown to halt addiction to cocaine, speed, heroin and alcohol, even after only one or two doses over a period of three to six months. It is used by tribes in the Congo for ceremony, visions, and the reduction of fatigue while hunting. In users, it also produces dream and out-of-body states, and an "oscillating sound." (*Nexus* magazine, Aug-Sept. p. 27 from Howard Lotsof's website.) Ibogaine is not approved by the FDA.

Chapter 14

Soul And Software

"If you want your children to be brilliant, tell them fairy tales. If you want them to be very brilliant, tell them even more fairy tales."

–Albert Einstein

A women's magazine featured a photo of Marilyn Monroe on how she would have looked had she lived into her fifties. In the picture Marilyn looked nearly the same. The caption said that all the obligatory facelifts and reconstructions that stars receive had been figured in. I wondered, what was the point of the article?

How soon beauty fades in the biological world! But in South Carolina a cable channel uses a test pattern that shows tropical fish tank with water plants. The local cable station, named FISH TV, has received floods of letters of appreciation. The calming nature of the fish, and the low maintenance of the tank are quite popular. No one need feed the fish and so no fish die, to be scooped up and returned to the organic world. Someday you may be on Fish TV. Others will read your face, be soothed when you blink colors and universal images in response to a voice. You will communicate through an internet to the whole world; none will know if they see only your image (your body still whole and apart from the net), or if you are in fact only a cyborg. You too might forget—your brow will wrinkle on FISH TV, but not at all the "great wrinkled brow" of a whale like Moby Dick. Images are not necessarily imagination. The image of a dying whale in a computer is one thing, but a dying whale in the sea, or in the mind is . . .

An image becomes more when the mind projects true meaning upon it, when there is the power of reflection. Image alone is like raindrops on a window sill, or clouds gathering over a hill. Imagination is a thing of the underlying mind like the language of Robert Bly in his poetry: "It was among ferns I learned about eternity," or Linda Gregg's poetry: "I want Her always standing as beautiful as the power that makes lambs and birds."[1]

From an image, however, one may create imagination and true experience.

> She is given a violet
> and in the violet is the sun
> she is asked let the violet go
> so she closes her eyes
> her mind becomes a violet
> it holds the sun
> she sings in a forest of rich light

Imagination, the realm of artists and mystics, is where the germinating of beauty and ideas arise. Aircraft and the dissection of human anatomy were first explored by artists like Leonardo da Vinci. Also, the future is often imagined first by science fiction writers. Let us hope that imagination has a place in the programming of the new technologies. For a great danger lurks if humanity deifies computers and sets their children before it. In his book, *Magical Child*, Joseph Pearce writes about idiot savants who can compute mathematically in the quintillion range and with great speed, but without insight as to the meaning of their answers. Pearce stresses that idiot savants give answers; they don't offer questions.[a]

They play "perfectly" on an instrument after but one "hearing" of it. They do not creatively compose. High intelligence and deep feeling seem to be missing. Children who are autistic also seem locked into a box of perception. Nikos Tinbergan, Nobel prize winner in 1973, spoke of the epidemic of infant autism in all technological countries of the world.[3] So the question is, how are we "en-souling" our children? Shall we encourage them to click cursors with preset outcomes? Will computer light ever rival an Audubon light, full of untamed birds?

> She knew there was some truth in pretending,
> the mouth where amphibians land
> from this etherized distance she saw her body
> her brain was outside her mind
> she even imagined its posterior
> a wolf's tooth
> Nothing is happening, she started
> I will die of fiction, of boredom

The marketplace has already spawned games in the image of the military, like Battletech and Dactyl Nightmare, both virtual reality games. In Battletech, you can "walk" a robot on a far planet and make battle with the enemy. In other Virtual Reality programs, go up the steps of the Acropolis—not to meet Socrates, but to dodge behind columns, and vaporize robots coming out of nowhere. Or be bolder, be Bad Mojo in the Roach game and "enter a world of perilous puzzles and bizarre perspectives," as the ad reads.

But many cyber-machines of all kinds seem to promise mind expansion by their very names, like the Electronic Mind Pyramid and the Affordable Shaman. This is the first time in history where everyone is a shaman or an Egyptian immortal, or at least thinks they are. Just surf your way in—use a credit card. A high-lighted coming attraction is a witnessing of Christ's Crucifixion. A woman in the eastern United States is presently planning construction on the Station of the Crosses. The visitor walks through a mall which has shopping stalls similar to those in Jerusalem during Jesus' time. The visitor then passes each station of the cross. The last stop is in a room where the Crucifixion takes place in virtual reality form.

Some will ask, where is the whole body, the individual mind? "For as a snare shall it come on all of them that dwell on the face of the whole earth." (St. Luke 21:35). The central computer of the world is already in Belgium. Some say, order has come at last to the world.

> She wonders, whom is she a copy of?
> a cell divides into blue
> copies itself
> learns immortality,

A computer image cannot substitute for soul. A computer robot is not a friend.

VIRTUAL HIGHWAY

> The highway clicks along like a cursor
> the desert ahead cut to the color of watermelon
> but we are talking blue mountains
> my holofriend and me
>
> I drive and she reads
> the Virtual Times,
> she reads the paper as if
> it were a flower
> and she a bee
> delving over and over
> for the sweetest news
>
> blue skies and holocreeks
> we head toward the mountains
>
> but I think it will sting her heart
> if the edge has gone too far
>
> I touch the cursor
> and pencil in a face
> for one I needed more

Computer romance may be as risky as that in real life, for distance makes the heart fonder. An e-mail rose beckons in the shiny screen.

ALPINE

She stands
on the white
staircase
like solemn glass

she waits
as if frozen
for him
to tap the pane

she thinks,
those lips could kiss anyone
and they are warm when
the trees are warm

she slowly
descends the stairs
her glove
lightly touched
with frost

she looks
but he is not there
he hides in wind

The pane is shiny black
it mirrors her, the stairs
and the bolts of wind
that close this night

The Green Revolution of the 1960's and 70's experimented with computer models of rice growth using Apple programming and the University of Southern California. The Green Revolution was in tandem with the United Nations Food and Agricultural

Organization, and the promise was for faster growing rice to feed the millions in Indonesian cities. Researchers studied the rice growth of the traditional long-cycle Bali rice as compared to a faster growing short rice. The new rice strains, however, required pesticides for prodigious yields, so chemical pesticides were sold at subsidized prices. At first, the short, fast-growing rice was a success. But since the 1970s, an explosion of plagues and rats has taken over the rice paddies. The traditional Balinese method of farming called the Temple System, has worked for generations and without the problem of pesticides and plagues. This system yields the largest amounts of rice over time with the fewest pests. Farmers build shrines for goddesses where water enters a field. Natural pulsations of the water are linked with nutrient flow cycles of the ecology. This system is more strained in modern times since tourism has arrived and other commercial interests. The advice of imported experts has been to dismiss the Temple System as a "rice cult." The southern tip of Bali, an island featuring luxury hotels, uses large amounts of water. It has become a political issue although tradition holds that no matter how many kingdoms are at war, the island farmers can continue to feed the people. Farmers thus remain independent of Bali's political arenas.

German women flock to Balinese men. Balinese men are artists, and they wear a flower in their hair. If a woman becomes pregnant, the man always weds her, as an ancestor is coming through and one cannot leave an ancestor in the lurch. There is always enough for those being born. There are thirty-plus fruits. There is no crime, although two areas have been sacrificed to tourists. But even rude tourists become softer after hanging out with these island people. No one would think of hurting another in this yielding gentle place.

Marlo Morgan, author of *Mutant Message Downunder*, gave a talk here in Santa Fe. She spoke of a banquet that a group of Australian aborigines invited her to. She had helped numerous aborigine youths to develop work in the cities of Australia. She was quite excited and chose a special dress for the occasion. An English speaking aborigine met her to drive her to the banquet. He told her that she had agreed to this meeting before she was born. Marlo did not know what that meant at the time. As the road continued into Australian outback, the intense heat made her uncomfortable in her stockings and party-wear. Unknown to her then, she would soon be walking barefoot for three months with several adult aborigines and her one interpreter. She would learn to eat snakes, maggots, lizards. She was chosen to take the message to the world. The message is that mutants, meaning us, have forgotten our spirits and who we are. The aborigines call themselves the Real People. They said of mutants "You have lost your smell of flowers and we think that you are probably from outer space."[4] They feel sorry for us. Each morning, the group chants and sends out thoughts to the animals and plants in front of them saying, "Sixty-three people are walking your way. We are coming to honor your purpose for existing." They would sing songs of the earth, and heal broken bones. Marlo witnessed a man's bone heal incredibly fast. They said they "jog the memory" of the bone into acknowledging the nature of its healthy state. Healing and disease take place, they say, in an instant. They communicate psychically, but say that we are as magical by dropping quarters into phone booths. They have nothing to hide in their thoughts. There is not enough food lately for this group, nor for the next generation. In the past they stayed in a cave, a place that has kept the people alive since the beginning of time, even when the Great Flood was here.

The Real People are leaving the planet; a third of the group has already consciously died, but they are not sad. They go on in the Forever. They say they are the direct descendants of first beings, and there are many places in the universe that souls like us can take on body forms. Their message is also that they can no longer help the mutants, who must stop destroying the soul of the earth. And how do they find what they need? Marlo found water by being water. Beingness.

In Santa Fe, at the hospital where I work, an Intensive Care Unit Registered Nurse spoke of her experience in an Australian hospital where a pregnant aboriginal woman wandered in. After delivering her baby, the woman appeared lost in the square building and halls. She left without her baby. Probably very sad, she was able to find her way back over a familiar 1200 miles in the Outback to her clan. The baby may be a gift to mutants.

Note:

—The author thanks Microsoft Word and Windows '95 for a technology that aided so much in the preparation of this manuscript.

Ancient herbs were discovered via trial and error. The principles of sympathetic magic were based on a search for similarity between human and plants, when humans felt themselves as a part of nature. The way plants grew mirrored actions in the body.

—from a student's herbology notebook

The Swamp Cooler

The first thing I noticed that July morning was the clumped coffee grounds in the can. The humidity had also soddened the page I was typing on; in fact, my letter was limp over the typewriter. The swamp cooler was obviously doing its job! We were the only people in Florida we knew who did not have a conventional air conditioner from which harmful fluorocarbons are released into the atmosphere. While I patted the letter dry, my husband teasingly reminded me that writing environmental letters might have to wait until winter in this climate. "After all," he said, "evaporative coolers work best in dry regions like Arizona. We live in Florida." Admittedly, we were nearly drowning in the humidity it produced. Our young son, Jon, had even donned a scuba mask and fins to sweetly illustrate this fact, the droplets faintly streaming down the glass in front of his nose and eyes. I laughed, then gently tossed him the rest of a cantaloupe rind, "Here, sweetie, eat this, and you can't eat with that glass in front of your face." He removed the mask, and began chewing with the side of his mouth along the peel. Meanwhile, my husband had decided to crawl up to the swamp cooler to make sure it was filtering properly. He said it sounded like an obscene loud cricket up there. When he returned he was holding up a dirty sneaker he found in the water tank. This was an irony, we thought. While preserving clean air for others, our own air had become mildly polluted by a stray sneaker. A week after that we'd gotten more used to the moisture. We made the best of it, softly punctuating our conversation with comments like "That cooler has made all the difference. It is like Venice without the pigeons." Then one day while straightening the neckties in my husband's closet, like picking off green garden snakes, I noticed actual puddles of water on the closet floor. There were mysterious streakings through it, the color of dark teal. It felt odd, as if I were looking at a private breeding ground. I suggested that we all go outside for regular air, at least for a short while. Soon we were in the kitchen packing picnic lunches of bologna and plenty of cold fruit. We were having fun, really, making a game of who would open the front door and walk out into the heat first.

When we did step out onto the concrete, and looked into the eyeless sky, we were both numb and alert, like the moment before an anesthetist's mask descends. A somnambulant breath had left clouds suspended and faded. The trees were in a haunting quiet, and under each limb was the tree's dark form. Our own dark forms moved slowly down the street past the last houses.

Inside the park area, black sweat cooled the vegetation. Jon noticed the reflection of the plants on our sunglasses. He removed his own sunglasses to be used as a mirror he could place against several kinds of plants. He said he was seeing himself! We said that was fine except that we were having a hard time finding a picnic spot. It was a swamp of spidery growths, indiscriminate oozings, and the baggage of flapping predators overhead. It was a thousand eons ago and it was vaguely familiar.

We became sad about ever finding a picnic spot. Our eyes held a moisture apart from the swamp, which was a past fragment that could never move on this land. Hearts groaned against sternums. Steam hung heavily as sloths. Ant-like wings hammered like a verb. Most insects did not fly but hobbled over mud and entered holes by habit. Limb to limb the vaporous fade of sun and insects. We must climb higher and get out, simply go on banging on the senselessness, and know a flower does not turn from the sun, as we could not turn from our mirror-like glasses.

Our march continued. The swamp was getting on our nerves. We were nearly blinded from staring at so much mud. We saw odd shadows moving torporously up certain trees. We all stepped back at once when we realized the shadows were catfish. Jon pointed to a nearby lake from which we assumed the catfish had hatched. The highway, far off, sounded hypnotic, dreamy, yet moving fast toward an edge. A fat mosquito. The low tide spilled a sludged gar. The inkiness on our shirts! The lake didn't say a word. A pupil drinking in. We nearly lost patience, waterbugs scribbling like a bad temper.

My husband said if he heard another frog jump, he'd break its legs. I looked at the sky and said, "I damn you all."

We were so spent by it all the belly of things could make us cry. We decided the swamp was a wound with nothing to say to us. We became sleepy, the kind of sleep willed on slave ships that return one home. But we needed to press on. In order to not call attention to ourselves, we smeared muck on our faces.

We became dark and powerful. We did not jump from things, but instead stood on long, firm legs. Nascent memories were crawling in the bog and into us. There was one moment when all was absolutely still, and the insects stopped and we felt watched. I dared not say that it was the eerie silence in woods when all creatures know a wild man, or hominid, or Bigfoot, is nearby. This moment passed. We then attracted unusual things. A cloud of plumed moths were suddenly fanning us. We were cool and happy. We knew our power and looked around for something to worship.

Broken Spell

Emily expected the phone to ring soon. She sat at the long kitchen table, its glass panels, now blue and rosy, watery looking, reflecting the afternoon sky. She spent many hours at this table, picking up light, her mind deep in photosynthesis. Her life was scheduled around arousing without alarms or day shifts. Being artistic, she started each day with a kind of awe, a putting on of animal skins, first for dramatic impact and only later for warmth.

On most days, her ritual began when she rose before noon barely out of REM. She began the coffee, but drank only the fresh ground kinds. Waiting for the Italian roast and her mind to kick in, she would stare at the light on the panels. Emily was really a very easy to please person who attended to her own needs quietly and privately. There were only rare intimations to others, her friends, the public, of how fragile her life would be, of how totally in crisis it would be, if her mid-morning ritual were taken from her. Emily's heart was the type that easily laughed, but finding her bearings was a delicate maneuver.

Around her kitchen were lemons, oranges, and paper napkins that appeared to her aesthetically placed. Today was another perfect moment, the shape of high-keyed birds. The telephone rang. Phone in hand, Emily swiped the table with a peach cloth to maintain its shiny reflections. She listened to Diane, loved her ability to add mystique and aristocracy to her experiences.

Then Emily intoned, "I went to a workshop. I was both the woman giving birth, and the infant being born."

"We must meet for coffee!"

"Oh, let's!"

At the sidewalk cafe, blue plates and cups were already set out on white linen. Orange slices and lemon misted the air. Diane said, "Marge is sending invites for a croquet party for beginners. Do wear croquet attire. We might as well go all out! We'll start early in the morning, and have a continental breakfast." Emily tried to organize her thoughts. She tried to picture herself among landed gentry on a green estate in culottes, self-consciously swinging a mallet, then hurrying to keep up with the pack ahead.

"Emily, are you coming?"

Oh God, thought Emily, that question.

"I wish I could get around to these extra curriculars. The days go so fast."

"I know you don't care," replied Diane with a quick smile.

"It isn't that I don't care." Emily thought to herself, how can they plan their days around such mindless activities? The truth is, they don't care about my higher endeavors!

Then Marge arrived, waving up the sidewalk, "Hi, hey you two, this croquet game is a fund-raising. It will be fun—finger snacks, a raffle, and a band!"

Emily waved back, then tucked her poem under the table.

> A woman writes, "All things pass away.
> So shall I.
> A blue flower over a knife
> finds its face in silver
> perhaps on a palette."

Marge, a large woman, sat across from Emily, and announced, "Croquet is really a social skill, a game with intriguing history."

"I'd love to read about it sometime," said Emily.

"Show up this Saturday bright and early. We expect you."

"That's nice, but I'll be doing my art."

"This is one day, Emily. And a skill. A social skill."

"Beethoven wrote music without social skills," Emily blurted, embarrassed at having to defend herself so sophomorically.

"In fact, his lack of social skills kept distractions at bay."

Marge laughed, "He could have had it all, symphonies and a life. Who needs another symphony?"

"Who needs another croquet round? And besides, writing a symphony isn't a skill, or else they'd be churning out Mozarts and Beethovens and Jimi Hendrixes. Not to say formal schooling isn't necessary." Emily thought, this is getting stupid.

Diane remarked, "That is interesting, with all the music schools."

"It's a bit chilly. How about a warm-up?" asked the waiter.

"Yes, please."

People began to don sweaters. A small breeze lifted the corner of her napkin, and across the street, a slender stream was moving, beautiful as a water moccasin.

"It's getting late."

The sun began to slant, creating soft pink shadows off adobe walls. The sunset hung with the shapes of torn clothes. Emily thanked Diane and Marge for the visit. Emily made sure her friends were safely in their cars. She strained her eyes until the cars drove out of sight, for friends are the wayward flowers. And turning, she knew their wishes, heard the snow moan in the river's past.

Emily would attend the croquet fund-raising. She saw herself on the greens, swinging the mallet after an orange ball, or chasing it into green hedges glinting in the sun.

Then Emily looked for her own car. The sun seemed to have suddenly flown away. She thought of a quote from Chekhov, who said of this level, everything is forgiven, and it would be strange not to forgive.

Chapter 15

Chaos And Its Forms

"Leaves are not more shed from the trees, or trees from the earth, than they are shed out of you."

–Walt Whitman, "A Song for Occupations"

There is an evocative language that refers to nature. Called chaos, its patterns are "butterfly effect," "strange attractors," and "infinite nesting." It is a language that goes beyond the ancient idea of sacred geometry in that it is non-Euclidean, fractal, and its calculus mathematical expressions include not only a stable order but a universe that changes, grows and moves. Nature is always creative, each thing is subtly different—each snowflake unique. I am reminded of Job 38:22 when God asks, "Hath thou entered into the treasures of snow?"

A friend, Bill, wanted the newly picked pears sorted into two groups, one tart and the other sweet, for more homogenous preserves. He asked his wife, Joanne, to sort the pears. But to her husband she replied, "Why would I want to sort pears? I'd have to sort as many piles as there are pears." Joanne said a profound thing. Nature does not separate the wheat from the chaff as we do out of some unexplained odd purpose. A single pear may grow up unpredictably, yet within a sort of boundary. A particular pear arises from a species that is bounded by certain characteristics. The pear falls into this finite boundary. Each pear is individual in some way from all the other pears. No fructologist can predict its every mark. No two pears are exactly identical, but no pear becomes an apple, ever.

Nature loves variety, infinite colors and tones, the result being that all creations are individual, even if within certain boundaries. In chaos theory, the butterfly effect is "sensitive dependence on initial conditions." This means that a tiny variation in input can greatly effect the outcome. That is, a slight warming trend in Bali might result in a glacier inching forward in Washington State. Or a small doodle on scrap paper may spawn a revolution in a few years. "Infinite nesting" refers to the natural tendency to replicate. Lightning bolts branch into more refined bolts that mirror the parent branch. The ancient Etruscans, a sensual and artistic people, understood intuitively what chaos theory is, and developed to the highest degree the interpretation of thunder—and named the many gods that hurled lightning in a myriad of ways. A person or a society may be caught up in a "strange attractor." A strange attractor denotes that every system is attracted to a particular end state, moving erratically yet within certain parameters or boundaries. A person or society may become caught in a constructive or destructive attractor. God is the ultimate strange attractor.

Just before World War II there was a party in Chicago, and all hoped to hear the fight of Irish heavyweight Jack Doyle. While clapping and whistling at the radio, no one at first noticed they had tuned in by mistake to the deadly cheering and applause from a Nazi rally in Berlin. Any media, and computers, can be a strange attractor plugging all into a coded language that takes you where the program and its merchant so wishes. Symbols or anti-life symbols. But a software writer and lover of Liberty, Philip Zimmermann, has written a program that is essentially uncrackable, named PGP for Pretty Good Privacy. This encryption, a complex algorithmic code, has been given freely through world wide computer networks in order to free the world from the tyranny of a central computer. PGP makes spying on foreign governments and citizens virtually impossible (and vice versa). The code is classified under "munitions" in the Arms Export Control Act, making its export without a license a felony, although Zimmermann is not being prosecuted, however, for reasons not given. Zimmermann says of the Feds, "They're treating us (citizens) like an enemy foreign population."[1] The federal alibi for their invasion of our privacy is the threat of pedophilia, as if only they can protect children (Waco being an example).

The future is not ultimately predictable, and individual deviations are powerful. In Chaos theory, all may appear to go along a rather smooth predictable path, a daguerreotype, a picture of you forever. But then, like erratic weather, there is a bump into something novel. The result is a bifurcation, a spin-off which leads to chaos, to a new direction of activity and energy. New orders of the universe are discovered; inner childlike wonder awakens.

> I knew when the day began
> It was with the first child to wake up
> like the first apple to drop
> in a heavy orchard

A society or person may need a nudge into a new pattern for a higher order of harmony, a kind of shamanism, to manifest. But while in the period of unfamiliar chaos, life is like a carnival of strange masks. A search for new meanings and symbols begins. While I was working on the psychiatric ward, I recall a young schizophrenic man in chaos who would look into a hallway mirror repeatedly to see if he existed, to find a self amid the chaos. Another patient, a woman with multiple personality, who thus had several egos, struggled with the sense that she sometimes did not exist, or was out there in lost time, a bird hesitating between songs in the sky. Entering chaos is a way to see into nature, into the nature of ourselves, a zoom lens—a moon that hangs in the closer sky, a beautiful, hypnotic and psychedelic eye. A patient came to the psychiatric ward one summer with the complaint that he was unable to reach the plaza all day, though he had been walking since dawn. He claimed he kept merging with trees. He was schizophrenic, and some of us envied him during his bliss states. But mathematician

Dan Winter warns: "After Kundalini magnetism washes your body, you will go insane if you do not move to a magnetically fractal neighborhood."

Chaos is not disorder in the deepest sense, but a part of nature. One tunes one's eyes and ears a little differently. Marilyn Monroe, not a musician, was able to comment to the pianist, "That's what they call classical music. I can tell because there isn't a vocal." Ravel's well-known "Bolero" is really a chaos song. "Bolero", a slow chaos, starts and goes by itself. Each phrase is repeated with a new instrument running through it, and musical layers added on. "Bolero" in the march of colors to the sun. Ravel said, "I have written only one masterpiece . . . Unfortunately, it contains no music."[2] Ravel thus issued a warning to the audience about this piece which lasts seventeen minutes and consists of "orchestral tissue without music." At its premier in 1928, a woman in the audience screamed that the composer must be "a madman."[3] It takes time for neurons to adapt to novelty. Decades later, the Beatles would have the same effect on audiences.

Chaos happens in nature, so what about in our brains? Conventional EEGs (electroencephalograms) are two-dimensional; they only measure summated extracellular voltage potentials of the surface of the neocortex. Scientists have mapped the cortex in three dimensions. The waves looked chaotic, like the surface of an ocean with little waves in big waves. The top four to five cells of the brain are closer to the physical universe than to the mental universe.

> sun blooms from the stalk
> white geese beat softly through the clouds
> is this how your own heart moves?
> but you will have to look close

Looking close, the most complex fractal, or chaos figure in all of mathematics, is the Mandelbrot Set. The Mandelbrot does not itself occur in nature but is used to study the growth of plants, the shapes of seacoasts and clouds. The Mandelbrot set has both finite and infinite characteristics. The heart-shape remains the same but its edges vanish off into infinity. On the edge of the figure, when magnified, one sees the parent heart shape repeated, though not exactly. The square root of negative one is a number one can use to derive the above effects. Negative one is called an imaginary number, and is also the number for imaginary time used by Stephen Hawking to describe the real time of the universe. The Mandelbrot set describes worlds within worlds (infinite nesting).

> (The square root of negative one is one of the five transcendent numbers: negative one, one, zero, pi, and i. To create a Mandelbrot set, begin with a number and square it, then add a constant to it which gives a new number. Take the new number, square it and add a constant and get a new number, et cetera.)

The Mandelbrot set itself does not appear in Nature, but curiously the M-set did appear in the form of a crop circle on August 12th, 1991 near Ickleton in Cambridgeshire, Britain. Discovered by a pilot, the formation was mysteriously burnt two days later by persons unknown.

The Mandelbrot set is a form of symmetry and asymmetry, and is both an "artificial" and mental construct as well as a mathematical matrix behind nature. The embedding of worlds within worlds signified by the Mandelbrot set is symbolic of ourselves in the world of atoms within and the galaxies without. In nature and supernature geometry ratio (especially the golden mean) and not scale is what is important. Thus, in a near-death experience, the departed soul may be to us "nowhere," so small is its scale. But to that soul, we are in the small space, as it unfolds into other dimensions. To be conscious and have eternal memory is to be in ratio, to touch all enfolded space, which is the unified field.

Chaos is the way into nature and worlds beyond, a unified field. Chaos is a link to eternity. A metaphor would be to stand in a forest, and ask, more than how much lumber can be cut from an acre, and instead go further, asking, how many board feet are in a beautiful forest?

When we are in a Newton box, or are being watched while in an isolated part of nature, visits from outside are alien. In the 1950s, a child named Ron McAtee, who was in elementary school at the time and on a playground, saw in the sky a ship: "The ship was completely silent, yet there was an awful symmetry to the configuration of the ship, like it did not belong at all here. And yet there was a

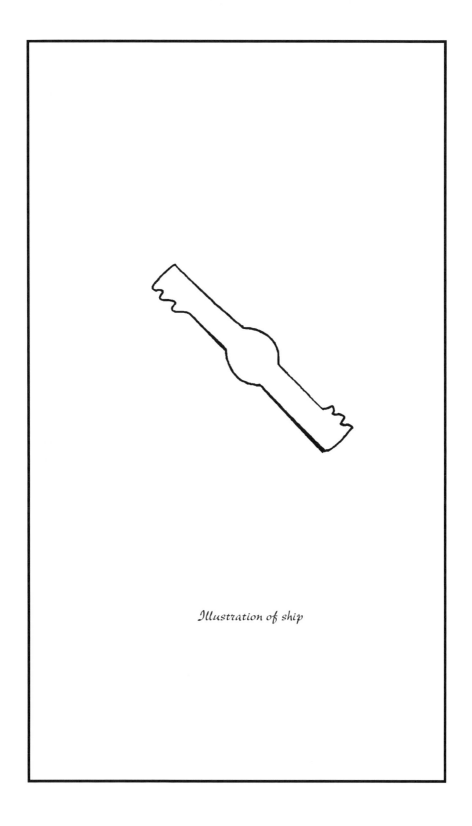

Illustration of ship

magnificent beauty to it all, actually beholding the art of another world."[4] The "rotor began to rotate around the sphere of the ship faster and faster until the ship just seemed to shrink and disappear." From the description of the ship he gave, its rotors appear to be a shape that could form crop circles (see illustration).

The mind recognizes perfect symmetry, but nature is more asymmetrical. Autistic children are so symmetrical that they are not attuned to variances of nature and chaos. One young autistic knew all about water heaters. He knew every detail about every brand of water heater, but his world was a water heater he could not exit.[5] Autistics, in their extreme symmetry and lack of spontaneity, tend to die young. Chaos is a way to break out of old patterns and rigidities. Extreme symmetry is an old state of being. The origin of the universe began in symmetry, and what we see now are the "broken symmetries."

Chapter 16

The Universe:
Sound

Open the bells that are us
the collisions of life!

You will not fly into pieces,
for you know in the beginning
All is welded to God

so go, and love atoms

—Angela Menking

Broken symmetries—melodies that branch off the original song. A woman told me a true story of a small flock of birds that alighted on her window sill every morning. Each morning began with a melody, birds and light—a career of colors. The woman would then listen for the song, but once she memorized it, the melody would change. The universe mind ever creates, but sometimes the music is mysteriously silenced. The Egyptian Colossi of Memnon, named by ancient Greek travelers for a Trojan hero, stand on the Nile flood plains near the Valley of the Kings. These two Colossi, each seventy feet high and cut from a single stone, were built for the mortuary temple of Amenhotep III (1411-1375 B.C.). One statue is called "the singing Memnon" because at one time in history, human voices and harps could be heard from it at sunrise. But in A.D. 202, the statue would not speak to the Emperor Septimius Severus and he tried to remedy the problem by repairing its cracks. However, the singing Memnon has never again been heard, although new cracks have multiplied.[1]

Sri Aurobindo spoke of the "genius of titanic silences" in his great poem Savitri. It is a silence of inner knowing beyond the forms, not a silencing of the creative forces of the universe. In Iran, the Ayatollah Khomeini, in an attempt to preserve a uniform, conformist society, outlawed all music but traditional Iranian music. Jimi Hendrix, the 1960s avatar guitarist, said in an interview, "I wish they'd had electric guitars in cotton fields back in the good old days. A whole lot of things would've been straightened out."

The ancient Etruscans' love of music is shown in a fresco in a tomb near Orvieto in which a piper plays as a baker mixes a batch of dough. The Etruscans played music to a multitude of activities such as cooking, walking, gardening, making battle, and sadly, beating slaves.

Singing is very inherent to learning. In Africa, a missionary noticed that the African children she was teaching seemed unable to add simple mathematical sums. But when the children sang and danced, they instantly arrived at the correct answer.

Australian aborigines sing over the land of the Creator, or else they say the land perishes. The song lines measure the land, having up to 100 verses, with each phrase and each pause exact in order to sing one from location to location. The landscape of human beings is also sung; even fractured bones have moved back into alignment, to the memory of wholeness, when an aborigine sings over them. Chinese intellectuals who were put out in the fields during the Cultural Revolution sang and recited poetry to recall acupuncture meridians. The names of acupuncture and moxibustion points are evocative, even poetic: Hidden White, Stomach Granary, Thought Refuge, and Pass Rush. A student was also expected to know the classics and literary allusion in order to understand relationships of energy. The energies in the body-mind connection cannot be grasped by rote, and are expressed best in art form.

When humans lose the song, and the intuition, they go maximal with the physical apparatus. West of Soccoro in New Mexico is the Very Large Array (VLA), twenty-seven dish shaped antennae that face up like shiny flowers toward the sky, collecting inaudible sounds. They spread across twenty miles, taking radio photographs of the sky. The weight of each antenna is 235 tons, which includes a huge reflector, eighty-two feet in diameter, with aluminum panels formed into a parabolic surface. The antennae catch radio waves as short as one centimeter, emitted by celestial objects. The intercepted waves record the creation and destruction of stars and galaxies. These inaudible radio waves are combined (all the antennae together) to simulate a single radio telescope which is the size of the entire array. The antennae may be packed together, or as far apart as twenty miles.

The array, in haunting patience, collects for intelligent sound on the San Augustin plains. Ironically, on these same plains, in July 1947, an alleged alien saucer crashed (further west than the Roswell UFO incident).

Astrophysicist and musician Dr. Fiorella Terenzi visited the VLA to classify celestial objects aesthetically. She created a sound synthesis program to bring the radio wave emissions of celestial objects into the sphere of human hearing. Her background includes voice, opera and piano. Her 1991 debut recording, *Music of the Galaxies*, contains the unaltered sound of galaxy UGC 6697. The music has been described as "ethereal and sensual, transporting the listener into a hypnotic state."[2] Her next recording will include the sound of the rings of Saturn.

The unborn fetus already responds to music while in the womb, preferring a light Vivaldi over the heft of Beethoven. Infants, like early mankind, have a softness on the top of the head. The fontanels, thick fibrous membranes that unite the bones of the baby's skull, completely ossify by eighteen months. The suture lines, the thin fibrous tissue that connects the fontanels, however, do not completely close until one's mid-twenties or early thirties. The fontanels are the large diamond shape area on an infant's head—as if a fount of light could emanate.

We are born remembering who we are, but quickly forget. The Hopi Indians say that early mankind kept the door open to the Creator through this spot by singing. If anything goes wrong, the Hopi say, the universe will sound a warning.[3] In Revelation 8:1, there is an eerie silence of a "half hour" in heaven before all hell breaks loose.

A woman visiting friends in the Mediterranean took a walk one evening, very happy and singing to herself, when she "heard the sound of evil." She stopped a moment, "frozen to the ground." Then, "an angel took me up under my arms, it was pure love, and carried me to safety." When she returned to her friends, shaken, she decided not to talk about the experience, and instead she joined in a game of charades! But her friends noticed the bright light around her, and she told of what she encountered.

In Sanskrit, the primary level of the world is the sutra, or thread. In order to have the physical world, a consciousness must sound the energy into form and matter. The sound "om" opens the chakra wheels, the vowels canter into fields of heaven. In modern physics theory, trillions of superstrings in the universe vibrate, turn into space and time, and all its manifestations. Superstrings can only be imagined in the mind; the prefix "super" means that these strings reside far beyond the fourth dimension (up to the twenty-sixth, but most comfortably on the tenth). Vibratory rates crystallize into things—trees, moths, raindrops. But when all crystalline nature is tuned to light, the sound of God, the Hu, is heard. This ultimate resonant harmony is the sound that makes us "Hu-man."

Notes:

—Our cerebral hemispheres are not particularly in synch. In Hemisynch®, the halves of the brain act in unison to "hear" a sound that the whole brain will hear, generate. This synchronization is reported to decrease symptoms of schizophrenia, decrease perception of pain, to help overcome jet lag in pilots, and even invoke Out-of-bodies. Robert Monroe, well known for out-of-body travels, developed tapes that isolate one ear from the other, so that separate sound impulses are sent to each ear and a third is created by the brain.

—Hallucinating people, like schizophrenics, are not "talking to themselves." Imaging via PET scanners has demonstrated that during an hallucination, although the areas of the brain related to hearing light up, the areas for speech do not light up. God or archetypal beings may be communicating to schizophrenics with some autonomy.

Chapter 17

Space, Time, And God

"The two who are made of Truth yet made of magic have come together; they have made a child and given birth to him and made him grow. He is the naval of all that moves and is firm, who with his mind stretches the thread of the poet."

—Rig Veda

"So he drove out the man; and he placed at the east of the garden of Eden Cherubims, and a flaming sword which turned every way, to keep the way of the tree of life."

—Genesis 3:24

"I believe in things seen and unseen."

—from the Nicene Creed

A new theory of consciousness states that the brain has a scanning system that sweeps across all areas of the cerebral cortex every 12.5 thousandths of a second.[1] The scan takes the form of a wave of nerve impulses sent out from a group of cells in the thalamus called the intralaminar nucleus. A 40-cycle-per-second wave continuously sweeps the brain from front to back every 12.5 thousandths of a second. The theory is that consciousness is a dialogue between the thalamus and the cerebral cortex. I thought of the sword of Eden, the dialogue between fallen man and God, and of consciousness keeping consciousness out of the garden, until we are ready.

I read an article, "Is the Photon Belt the Fulfillment of Prophecy?" by Patricia Diane Cota-Robles, which discusses a force-field/light-beam that our planetary system passes through in space every 12,000 years.[2] The period of 12,000 years seems to me a resonance with 12.5 thousandths of a second, the scanning period of the brain in the new theory above.

This photon belt may be but a beautiful myth, but it is a curious one that promises a new heaven and new earth when our Sun enters it. The photon belt is described as a huge torroid shaped ring composed of photon light particles near the vicinity of the Pleiades. The Pleiades, also called the Seven Sisters, is a cluster of stars in the constellation of Taurus 400 light-years from Earth. The largest and brightest of the cluster, Alcyone, was referred to as the "Central Sun" and "Great Intelligence" by the ancient Mayans. The myth says that the Pleiades is surrounded by a radiation belt (photonic) in the form of a disc similar to Saturn's rings, but which extends hundreds of light-years into space. Our planetary Sun passes through this disc every 12,000 to 13,000 years. It takes 2000 years each time to pass through the disc. Our sun completes one revolution around Alcyone in 24,000 years to 26,000 years. (A great zodiacal year is 26,000 years.)

Some surmise that Atlantis fell 12,000 years ago, but that its dawn was paradisiacal. Then increased materialism and forgetting of spirit transpired. This is part of a repeating cycle of paradises, then falls into veiled matter and darkness.

Every molecule that passes through the photon belt is affected. The photon belt's effects may be related to the extinction of dinosaurs, to ice ages, DNA mutations and to the nature of chakra systems. Passage through the Photon Belt may be divided into three sections. First is the null zone, which takes five to six days, and includes a period of total darkness for three days, if the pineal is not open. The three days of complete darkness and chaos were warned against in the Fatima messages. The next section is the main part, where daylight twenty-fours hours a day continues for 2000 years. This perpetual light radiates no heat, casts no shadows, illuminates even caves, or underground cities. In the book of Revelation there is a period of harmony and love, a New Jerusalem which has no sun, no stars, just perpetual light. (In Revelation it is a thousand years of peace. The photon belt ushers in 2,000 years of unique "light" and peace.) The last part of the belt ends as it began, with three days of darkness within a five to six day period. Our Sun and Earth may enter more obliquely and not have total darkness, but instead transform through a "slow transmission" and stepping up of energies.[3] If the earth enters the photon belt first, the sky will appear to be on fire, but this is a cold light without heat. If our Sun enters first there will be 110 hours of darkness and chaos.

We are due to enter anytime.

The entry into this belt that sweeps over our earth and heaven creates effects that are mostly at the level of psyche, for ninety percent of the photon belt is not of a physical nature in our terms. This belt is not the reason for Earth's geological upheavals, but it creates problems for electrical systems of all kinds. Time is experienced differently because one is outside the normal time and space experience of the former physical world. The new energy age becomes the Photon Age. The Photon Age may well be on the horizon.

Tom E. Bearden, a systems engineer, has released his work on photon energy free to the world through scientific bulletin board services. A member of the Association of Distinguished Scientists, he has worked as a consultant to the aerospace industry. He has bypassed governments and corporations, and offered humankind his work, "The Final Secret of Free Energy," in 1993.

A photon is a particle that is a constituent of light, X-rays, and other forms of electromagnetic radiation. It travels at the speed of light, has zero mass, no electric charge, and an infinitely long life. It is sometimes called a light quantum due its wave-particle characteristics. A photon light particle is the result of a collision between an anti-electron (positron) and an electron. This split second collision causes the two particles to destroy each other with the resulting mass completely converted into energy that registers as photons or light particles. There is no anti-particle to light.

Bearden writes: "empty space is filled with an incredibly intense flux of virtual particles." Space is a plenura of potential energies and forms; it is not empty space, per se. It is the "vacuum energy," where time does not exist, nor distance as we know it. The goal, he says, is to order the local force fields and he states one can do this with the mind as well. He is at work on the physics end, focusing on scalars, which are points in the space-time potential. A scalar is "hidden" in a quantity without a direction—the vector sum of a scalar is zero. Electrogravitation is caused by a very small scale curvature of space-time which produces enormous but randomly fluctuating force fields. (The beginning of the universe was a quantum flux.) He writes: "There is infinite energy in each of these enfolded waves and anti-waves, but in a localized region, the energy density wave is finite." The entire universe is filled with free energy and he claims, "God has been most kind."

Bearden's concepts are difficult for those schooled in traditional physics. His system works by basically oscillating the charge around an atom, and therefore "exciting" an electron into a higher shell, producing an increase in potential energy as the electron gathers energy from the vacuum. When the charge is cut off, the electron jumps back to its former shell and releases the stored difference in energy as a photon of electro-magnetic energy into the physical realm. The secret is to not permit a flow of electrons (electrical current).

Bearden writes on the "use of local finite mass collectors . . . to only dissipate energy from a collector, not a source." Creating current depletes a source. He advises to "collect the bountiful fruit from nature's tree, instead of chopping down the tree itself and killing it." That is, be in "harmony resonance" and do not create a current.

The world, claims Bearden, can be powered anywhere free with this energy using many variants of collectors with batteries for one's home, or business. It will only cost a few hundred dollars and generate sixty Hertz AC as long as one doesn't demand current (which is the rate at which the energy is being freed and dissipated). It will be inexpensive, non-polluting, and free.

The ancient Indian Vedics used language similar to Bearden's to describe energy. The Akashic Record stores information on all that has happened and it continually records. Akasha is Sanskrit for "space" which is not void, but a plenum of titanic forces and interacting energy fields, an undifferentiated and unmanifested light. Manifested matter is crystallized light, or the Sanskrit kasha.

What else will manifest as the photon belt sweeps by? I wonder if the increase in number and complexity of the crop circles is connected to deeper entry into the belt? A Logos intelligence and light seeding Earth for a new cycle. The plants of crop circles change in their very crystalline structure, and they have different, very high levels of energy compared to controlled plant samples. The crop circle plants have displayed growth rates which over time return to normal. With a full beam, perhaps a final manifestation will appear, and we will be in a new subtle physical form. The crop circles may be depicting a return through an aperture and back to the "emitter" of creation, my husband feels. (The term "emitter" derives from Robert Monroe's book *Ultimate Journey*.)

An anti-matter cloud may be sweeping over us. This foretells either of total, if gradual, annihilation or else a paradisiacal "concrescence" at the end of time.[4] In *The Invisible Landscape*, Terence and Dennis McKenna write of this collision wherein particle and antiparticle cancel each other out leaving only pure energy (photons). We will become unrecognizable to ourselves. The McKennas surmise this event will occur across the complete topology of the entire space-time continuum, and "not gradual but simultaneously something impossible in a three-dimensional collision . . . in a hologramatic situation, where photons would retain the structure they possessed in matter and its stereoisomeric reflection in anti-matter" (at variance with Einstein's relativity but not with Whitehead).[5] There will "not be a localized explosion, but a universe whose physical laws suddenly cease to operate."[6] That is, being in the vacuum, leaving the flux of particle existence, our photonic forms, or light bodies, will be "able for the first time to obey laws relevant to themselves as photonic holograms . . . A mutation from matter to photonic form as tremendous freedom."[7] Is this the marriage of the Lamb and the Bride, of night with the Sun?

THE NIGHT DRIVE

The farthest wind sighs
where the desert washes out

You are there.

That night drive knows me well
and streams like a star
falling back home

How many times have I turned around?

I can say I miss you,
only I know the skin beneath that skin
and I will love you
with the last edge of sun

Robert Monroe, author of *Far Journeys,* in an out-of-body journey, visited the future around the year A.D. 3000 North America is pristine wilderness again. Human beings can create wild rice (food) in their hands by will: "the mixture of physical and other energies that was now earth life . . . I found I was unable to determine where one began and the other left off."[8] He journals how at that time, humans may leave their bodies protected by energy egg-like domes, and all is conscious. A human soul in the year 3000 slips in and out of light-bodies like clothes, can even merge with blissful trees. After 3000, we are more human. Monroe found himself in a fully operational body as a twenty-two-year-old, though souls can use any body by then. He had his own youthful body. He was told by a woman, "You were always saying we were more than our physical bodies. Now it's the other way around. We keep telling the new ones they are more than their energy selves."[9]

Currently, there is an incarnation that is a promise of our future light and love. A young woman from India, Mother Meera, remains in trance continually. Many flock to have her look into their eyes, to be filled with bliss. Actual light has been seen coming from her face and hands. She is recognized by millions as an incarnation of the Queen of Heaven. A being of divine love, she also holds divine pain, but says she cannot share that pain with anyone.

Another divine human, Jesus, was known in India as the Great Demonstrator, the Master Teacher Ishi. His incarnation was to show that death is not the end to consciousness, and that love is the key. (It was not beneath him to first die like a man, however). Women flocked around him, and after his death they were said to have seen a vision of angels at the tomb of Jesus. These women, including Mary Magdalene and Mary, the mother of James, found the stone in front of Jesus' tomb mysteriously rolled away. Inside the tomb was a linen cloth, but the body was missing. Later, when Peter and

Cleopas walked to Emmaus, they did not recognize Jesus as he approached them after his death. The disciples thought they were seeing the ghost of Jesus. In John 20:19, Jesus appeared to his disciples "when the doors were shut" and he "stood in the midst." But when Jesus ate fish in front of them and broke bread, "their eyes were opened, and they knew him." Then Jesus "vanished" out of their sight.

Curiously, Jesus' transfiguration was a year before he was crucified. The apostles Peter, James and John saw that his face appeared different, and his apparel was shining. There also appeared Moses and Elijah, conversing. Then a cloud manifested and the apostles, fearful, entered it. Inside the cloud was a voice that said, "This is my son." The transfiguration was a preview to a resurrected body.

Jesus, a multidimensional being, while in his physical body, multiplied loaves and fish for a hungry crowd. From the plenum/vacuum energy, he created abundance. And he promised "greater works than these shall Ye do, because I go onto my Father."

The mystic Emanuel Swedenborg entered trances and visited the heavens. When adults go to heaven, they become like angels and become more youthful, "more and more towards the springtime of life."[10] He wrote that if an infant dies on earth, it goes to heaven and thinks it was born there. The infant then learns to walk without practice and learns the "interior speech."[11] In heaven, time and space is an interior state. In a Swedenborg heaven, watching a sun advance across the sky is related to a state of mind, for distance is no barrier in heaven.

It is a mystery why immortality is kept from us here on present earth. Reactivated by the photon belt, would we be immortal? The human lifespan was much longer before Noah and the Great Flood. Adam lived 930 years, Abraham lived 175 years, and Jacob's son, 110 years. In Genesis we have the intelligence of the gods but not their immortality. (Elohim as "shining ones" may not mean plural gods in Aramaic, as the use of "I" and "we" in that language was not necessarily our modern sense of it.) There is a theory that ancient astronauts tampered with humanity's genetic material so that we would be asleep to our true nature, and instead be custodial slaves/caretakers of the garden for the astronauts. (The tradition of slavery has continued ever since.) In Sumerian myths, some gods were enslavers but some gods aligned with Enki who wished to liberate humankind. In Genesis, the Elohim take earthlings to marry ". . . that the sons of God saw the daughters of men that they were fair, and they took them wives of all they chose." These "Sons of Revolt" were the original Brotherhood of the Snake before it too became debauched. We may still be under the manipulation of ancient human-gods. In Africa there are old gold mines going back thousands of years where human slaves possibly mined gold for the astronaut "gods," who used it possibly as an atmosphere protection, or as a superconductor material.

Traces of being asleep are possibly evidenced by the presence of inert genes/chromosome filaments (fifty percent to as much as ninety percent of our DNA is inert). Ninety percent of the universe is also inert in the form of dark matter that might light up if we did. Of course, nature does seem to thrive well even with "errors." But is it possible that much of our neocortex, the "Light Brain," is not activated?

> ". . . and now, what if he puts forth his hand and takes also from the tree of life, and lives forever?"
> —Genesis 3:22

Notes:

—The idea we only use ten percent of our brain has little, if any, scientific basis, but if the brain is understood as a holographic emitter, then we may be limited.

—Jesus appeared to many in his transformed state; he taught forty days (forty is a sacred number of perfection, transmutation) and performed many miracles. The apostles also performed miracles and preached in the Roman Empire. Peter was imprisoned, then saved by angelic intervention. James, brother of John, was executed.

—The Shroud of Turin has an imprint caused by intense radiation of the life energy of the body. It is thought to be a negative of Jesus (or partly the handiwork of Leonardo da Vinci centuries later!) after an intense transmutation of the molecular structure, even a space-time alteration. The physical body of Jesus was perhaps resurrected as a light body (thus the "missing" conventional physical body). If the shroud is not Jesus' then a copycat managed to transmute the fiber, to scorch it in an unexplainable manner.

—The thalamus gland is the relay station for most information in the brain. The hypothalamus regulates sex hormones, blood pressure, and body temperature, among many things.

—The Essenes were the only spiritual sect in biblical days in which women were equal to men. Jesus had many women disciples.

—Passage through the photon belt will alter cells, and genetics, wherein "light bodies" are more "stepped up" and vibratory bodies will manifest. Psychic abilities (with heart, hopefully) will increase. During transition through the null zone, meditation and prayer are essential in order to not forget who one is, because during this time the decrease in the earth's magnetic field, now approaching zero, can erase memory. The earth's magnetism is partly a byproduct of the "pressure of the Photon Belt," states Nidle and Essene in their book, *You Are Becoming a Galactic Human*.

—The stars of the Pleiades are Alcyone, Electra, Sterope, Taygete, Maia, Celaeno, and Merope. Alcyone, the sun considered the Great Intelligence by the Mayans, is located eternally within the photon belt/ring. Photons are like thought, as both cannot be pinned down in space/time/mass.

—The author wonders what kind of souls/children will arise if born while Earth is traversing the photon belt. Will these be children of the Blue Ray?

A Warning Regarding The Eating Of Gold:

Too much light is Luciferian. It is a burning bush without emotion, a God-like being that has thrown out inner light, has bedecked itself to glitter in this world and used its magnetics to draw others forcefully to it—a great empty seduction. It will eat you. The Luciferian rebellion was about "bending light outside our magnetic bodies," says Dan Winter, computer and sacred geometry expert. Eating gold for immortality, Winter warns, creates "wormholes, implosions in the bloodstream that electrically cancel emotions and promotes hive consciousness." In the past, gold-mining slaves were produced this way "by the Dracos." (Africa has extremely old gold mines).

At the close of this century, another kind of gold has been discovered, a holy of holies related to the physics of an atom's nucleus. This substance may open the emotions of unity with all things, and it possibly makes the human body a magic carpet. Use at your own risk.

Chapter 18

Manna In The 21st Century

The word "Man" is related to manas, and originally meant, "the one who thinks."

I first read of an internal manna in Gopi Krishna's book, *Kundalini for the New Age*. He wrote of seeing a white powder after being enlightened: "There is a subtle organic compound in the body that the nerves carry to and fro, after extraction from the organs and tissues, that supplies the vehicle through which the incorporeal pranic energy acts . . . It seemed as if every object on which I looked was coated with a thin layer of white . . . as if a very thin coat of powdered chalk had been applied over it."[1] The hidden manna is everywhere. Then I heard of a man in the West who discovered this manna in a substance that can be ingested—a physical material.

It is in the nature of Western culture to manifest technology that alters society and the individual. In this sense there would almost be a historical impetus for an individual to come along and invent the ultimate technology, that of transforming the very inner nature of humankind itself—and in a form that can match the acceleration of the times. The individual who arrived to offer humanity good magic, a lift to a higher potential, is a man living in the United States, a farmer having American know-how and genius who also happens to be a descendent of King David.

David Hudson, a very successful farmer and agricultural scientist, decided in 1975 to extract gold and silver from tailings from old abandoned mines to create a hard currency. He was disturbed by the fact that Federal Reserve notes devalue money, as they are not backed properly by gold and silver. When David did find gold and silver, a problem presented itself that was not to be solved for another nineteen years. What he possibly stumbled onto was the manna of the Old Testament that came by way of Egypt, and even the "hidden" manna of the Book of Revelation. It was named by ancients "the Bread of the Presence of God, the Semen of the Father, and the Golden Tear of the Eye of Horus." David has learned also how to forge and refine it, as did the ancients.

In the beginning, all David knew was that in the process of extracting gold and silver, a powdery white substance was also being recovered, and it interfered with the amount of gold and silver David could actually obtain. Chemists and labs worldwide in the United States, London, and the Soviet Union were at a loss to identify the substance. Using emission absorption analysis down to parts per billion, scientists could say how far apart the atoms were, but the substance evaded a conclusive identity, like a kind of magic, or alchemy. Emission spectroscopy and fractional vaporization, and metal separation techniques were used, but the material seemed to not follow any guidelines for a positive identification. Even the weight of the material varied. This substance could not be found on the Periodic Table. Using neutron activation, an analysis of the nucleus of the element itself was done. The conclusion was "no precious elements are detected." This defied all the laws of conventional chemistry. David was then told to get patents—he has patents pending on 12 new forms of elements (iridium, rhodium, gold) in their "high spin orbitally rearranged monatomic state." The monatomic system, not the same as radioactive isotopes, is very stable. David found that if one takes one gram of gold and converts it to the monatomic form, there is a transitional state where the gold first becomes hydrogen rhodide, or hydride oride. Then, if the proton is annealed away, the material goes snow white like bleached fluffy powder. David noted that the gold substance and other monatomic substances became white powder and were not like a metal anymore (though these can return to metal under certain conditions). Monatomic gold and the other monatomic elements don't combine with anything (nor does the philosopher's stone in alchemy). These elements weigh fifty-six percent of their original weight when they go to the white powder state. Finally, the material was compared to a superconductor due to its "loss" of mass (an oscillation of its matter between two dimensions), and to its "asymmetrically deformed high-spin nuclei." Studying the nucleus gave the key. (The nucleus is perhaps like the holy of holies.)

Superconductivity has been found to be a mode of communication between cells in the body. David has stated that this energy moves like "a stealth bomber," "it is there, but hard to read." Cows and pigs have the high-spin states of iridium and rhodium in their brain tissue (5 percent). The human being is even more a superconductor than most beasts of the field. We have a light brain, but we are asleep to our true nature.

In ancient alchemy the "white powder of gold" was the color of the philosopher stone. Ancients were said to be given this stone by the gods back in the Tigris and Euphrates Valley, which is where Eden would be located.

In Egypt, at Giza, the top of the Great Pyramid, surmises David, was a great ball of glass gold, a superconductor. Since the Great Pyramid was built on solid bedrock, the low frequency of the earth vibrations could transfer up to the gold ball and charge the superconductor, which glowed. The pyramid as superconductor also amplified the pharaoh's thoughts, and being telepathic, the pharaoh knew all lies and truths in the kingdom. But then, David relates, the fierce Amalakites arrived in Old Kingdom Egypt, and destroyed the temple and most everyone (the pharaohs were now nowhere to be found), except for some slaves. Then the Amalakites realized their error in destroying the knowledge of the people, so they mummified killed leaders of Egypt to call back the souls for information, but nothing happened. No bodies of Old Kingdom pharaohs or priests have ever been found. They were said to have ascended to heaven as immortals.

The Hebrews took this knowledge with them out of Egypt at the end of Old Kingdom Egypt (3200 B.C. to 2420 B.C., from Menes to Pepi II): Moses and his tribe fled to the desert circa 1300 B.C. (The Levi tribe was related to the tradition of priests who carried on government and religious conventions. But the order of Melchizedek was mysterious, without particular lineage. This order may have known about the white powder of Gold. Hebrews 7:16 identifies Christ as a priest after the order of Melchizedek).

In Old Kingdom Egypt, initiates who purified themselves received the substance which was the Bread of the Presence of God. Like the bride in the bridal chamber, they awaited the Heavenly Father, and the transformation into superconscious sons and daughters of God. They lived as immortals, even 900 years, after which they consciously ascended to Heaven.

The Hebrews, who lived in Egypt and were the metallurgists and artisans, were able to make the manna. Mt. Sinai's fire and smoke was a kind of forge where gold was purified into a white fluffy state—a white feather and a white dove. In the secrets of alchemy, we are fed by the dove, later called the Holy Spirit, which is not to be blasphemed. (The unforgivable sin, says David Hudson, is to know all things and to sin anyway, to be like Lucifer, full of light, but to choose to part with God.)

The Ark of the Covenant kept the stone and manna through which God spoke to the Hebrews and to Moses. Only the priests, being pure in heart, body, and mind, could approach the ark of the Covenant being. If impure, one would be in dissonance with the ark, and could die, as if by bolts of lightning, because a polarity and current would be set up in nonresonance (an energy flux would arise with real volts). That is, unprepared, you cannot see God's face and live. To approach the ark/presence of God in harmonic resonance was to be able to enter the holy place. The ark in Exodus behaves very much like a superconductor, and it levitates at times.

A rabbi told David that no one has known how to make the white powder of gold since the destruction of the first temple—Solomon's temple. The trouble began when a pharaoh woman from Egypt became pregnant by Solomon. The son, "impure" according to

Hebrew law (racial purity), was pressured to leave, to which Solomon suggested that all first sons of the Levites should leave as well. The first sons did all leave, and with them went the ark of the Covenant back to Egypt, since they were the sons of the priests.

A number of modern men and women have ingested the manna substance forged by David. It has been found to cure diseases, even end-stage cancer and AIDS. It potentially cures all diseases as it reconfigures the DNA and brings inert filaments to life. The glandular system is restored. Aging is reversed and one has the body and energy of an eighteen-year-old again. The pineal opens and one becomes telepathic.

The real reason, says David, for taking monatomic gold is for the superconsciousness it brings, for a change in the nature of humankind. More than healing, it is the key to becoming a son or daughter of God. But before taking this gold, one must purify oneself. A "dark night of the soul" is part of purification. One must want the consciousness and be prepared. The substance is powerful enough that one could die, or perhaps worse, attain certain psychic gifts without a pure heart (for this is an accelerated Kundalini).

David spoke in a lecture of one man who has started this Egyptian rite of passage. The man fasted and purified on only water for nine days with a high colonic, then for thirty days he received 500 mgs. of monatomic iridium and rhodium orally. (David is cautious about using monatomic gold because its full power is not yet known. Therefore he has experimented with iridium and rhodium because they are found more naturally in the body.) Monatomic iridium and rhodium, however, proved to be dazzling. After the first five days of taking the material, the man heard a roaring sound that was "as nectar." The sound, which has grown louder each day, is not irritating, because it is not through his physical ears. He hears the blissful roar day and night. He says the sound originates about eight inches above his head and vibrates down into his brain and throughout his body. I have heard that sound is the way the paranormal gifts will be given to humankind. In Revelation, trumpets sound to open up the chakra centers. David states that human means "the man who hears the hu." After sixty days, the man began having dreams, visions, and visits with angels. He described full body Kundalini arousals, and says that one would burn if they touched his skin. He is enraptured with oneness with all of nature, plants, animals, humans and angels. He is telepathic, and knows thought is faster than light. He sleeps about two hours a night and is fully refreshed. Being immortal means he lives outside of usual time and space; it is not a mere longevity of the animal nature of man. He lives in a state of consciousness where the veil to heaven and the Godhood is lifted. As an immortal, he is made of androgynous energies. An immortal "dies" consciously, "ascends to Heaven." An immortal may even raise the dead. A child may be born from a human immortal or mortal, but children are not necessary to replace death (which is sad, and with immortality there will also be fewer old couples savoring their last years together). However, the children will be conceived in light, like virgin births. That is, physical conception occurs as usual, but the fetus grows with cells perfected and with DNA portals open to the universal Being. Such a virgin birth occurred when Jesus was born, suggests David. Mother Mary and the disciples were, David shows, members of the Essenes and the Melchizedek priesthood. (Many Bible scholars disagree with David's assumption regarding the Essenes connection, in that no evidence exists concretely). Mary was raised as a true high priestess, lived in the temple "as a dove and was fed by an angel." Jesus was born perfected by the light. The Essenes were said to have had twenty-eight tons of gold and forty-eight tons of silver, and David's studies indicate a forge. The Essene community was also said to have had angels living in it.

Jesus was a full light being; his full transfiguration (St. Mark 9) appeared with Elias and Moses to James, Peter and John, wherein a voice came from a cloud saying, "This is my beloved son ; hear him."

David has referred to the book, *The Quantum Self*, by Danah Zohar (a woman with degrees in both physics and psychology), as a way to meld science and religion. She explains that God is in the vacuum energy, the zero-point, the scalar energy which is infinite potential and the underlying energy of the universe. Every nucleus runs on it. Any fluctuations within it create matter, thought, and a kind of separation from God. Thus, "in mystical terms, this splitting off might be equated with alienation, or The Fall. Such a Fall is the prerequisite of creation or knowledge but it means leaving the Eden of total fusion." Therefore, Zohar has the insight that dialogue with the vacuum is dialogue with God, a mystical experience.[2] David says, "when face-to-face with your God, you will be in the vacuum."

David is a twenty-first century Moses, leading the people to manna, bringing light down from Mt. Sinai. Becoming a full light being requires ten lunar months, or nine solar months. Then, one's abilities include levitation. One can walk on water. One may also bilocate using the light body. The nature of oneself is that the light body is in charge of the physical body. So much of humankind's history has been the inverted nature.

In Revelation 2:7, it says "To him that overcometh will I give to eat of the tree of life, which is in the midst of the paradise of God." To the 144,000 in Revelation is written: "And they shall see His face and His name shall be in their foreheads." "In their foreheads" means being in the place of the divine. (In contrast, the phrase "on the forehead" refers to the mark of the beast, which is the worship of a worldly external image.) These 144,000 who are in the Lamb's Book of Life (the restored genetic code?) may be persecuted by the antichrist. These may also be raptured because they are multidimensional beings without the usual physical limitations. This transformation, a resurrection to an immortal body, is mirrored in a restored genetics. (I am curious if our DNA, now a double-strand, will not become, as some new age authors have forecast, a twelve-strand configuration that forms a star of David geometrically.)

David foresees a time when manna is given to all who are ready. His vision is of a nation of true high priests and priestesses, and not a nation of self-appointed priests. He refers to the book of Revelation, describing the foundation of such a new Jerusalem as made of gold ("and the street of the city was pure gold"). David is refining his monatomic minerals and hopes to release them to all who want it. He has mortgaged his home and placed all his faith in spirit. He funds all his own research, or else accepts donations. He states that he also found out a curious thing about his roots via a relative who became a Mormon and researched the family tree—David is a direct descendent of King David, the father of Solomon.

> I, Jesus have sent thine angel to testify unto you these things in the churches. I am the root and offspring of David, and the bright and morning star.
>
> —Rev 22:16

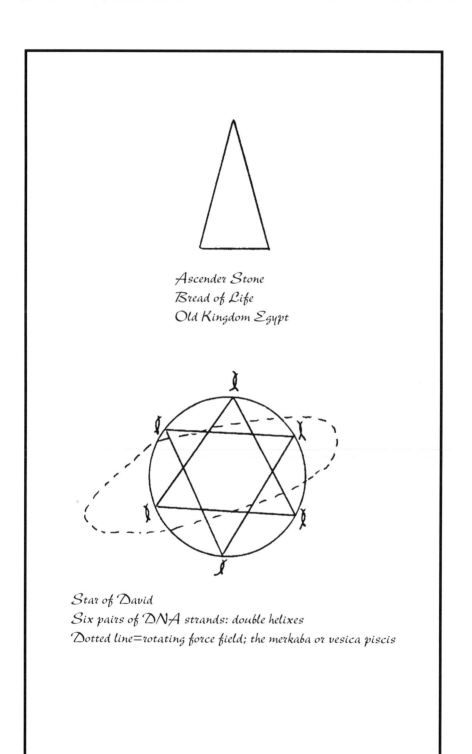

Ascender Stone
Bread of Life
Old Kingdom Egypt

Star of David
Six pairs of DNA strands: double helixes
Dotted line=rotating force field; the merkaba or vesica piscis

Notes:

—The white powder of gold is a full circle substance. When the ancients initially used it wisely, a golden age manifested. Then it was used for evil in the latter Atlantean times. Since the gold opens the psychic center, it allows the ability to move objects at a distance, or to "see" into homes, or affect unprotected minds; it could be used for mind control. Such an aberrant human would be created because the heart chakra was closed to spirit, or the fire going up the spine would encounter blocks and impurities in the body or soul. A premature transmutation can create a monster—and dark elementals.

A Lucifer can posture light and good, but is self-serving and externally controlling. Blasphemy of the spirit is when a being is full of light and knowledge and sins anyway. A Lucifer-type seeds black cubes of geometric destruction.

—In a superconductor is a single-vibrational frequency, like a laser, which flows perpetually in the system, but is without voltage or current. This resonance frequency tunes the wire so electrons vibrate at the same frequency as the superconductor; the electrons will pair up and go the path of least resistance, which is the superconductor. Superconductors don't have to touch if in resonance harmony; they flow light between them, unlike electrical circuits, which need wires touching. The nucleus can change its symmetry and electron orbital configuration and the electron positron pairs will form, which are light. Superconductors are extremely sensitive to any magnetism and will not break lines of magnetic fields, and will levitate instead. Gravity is the interaction of matter with the "zero point" or vacuum energy. There is no gravitational field, per se. When matter interacts between two dimensions—not three dimensions—and is resonance connected, it only weighs fifty-six percent of its true weight, as does the white powder of monatomic gold. David works to chemically obtain superconductive substances, whereas accelerators are used to create more current and focus on the charged particles, versus the superconductor field itself.

—Light is composed of photons, which have no anti-particle. There is no dualism in the nature of light. Light exists beyond space-time and cannot be knocked from one space-time to another. Light is what corrects DNA. A DNA "denaturing relaxation and recombination corrected" occurs when monatomic substances are given to the body, and thus messenger RNA can receive universal information via the DNA receptors and the body corrects itself.

—The manna of Exodus, which was not "hidden," may have been the fallen honeydew of aphids and their relatives, considered a delicacy in various parts of the world. In Exodus, the manna turns to worms if not picked in the morning for bread, but oddly, Moses' people were instructed by the Lord to gather twice the amount on the day before the Sabbath, and that manna kept fresh.

—Los Alamos National Laboratory in northern New Mexico has announced that superconductivity will be a reality in a few years, with superconducting power lines and magnetically levitating trains. Superconducting storage rings can carry over a million amperes of current per square centimeter of cross section. Ordinary copper wire of the same thickness carries under 800 amperes. The new tape is flexible and can be wrapped around objects as thin as a straw.

—There is a change in symmetry in nuclear configuration in a superconductor. The nucleus takes the shape of a football, or an arc/ark with a 2:1 ratio. A vesica pisces. (See my chapter on the Merkaba.)

—In monatomic superconductive metals, the nucleus, the single atom, has a temperature inside it that is nearly absolute zero—despite room temperature.

—The twelve tribes of Moses wandered for forty years in the desert. But there is as of yet no physical evidence of Moses and those years. Were they in three-dimensional time and space? If so, they moved their tents and made camps, following elaborate orders from the Lord, a distance comparable to a city wandering from the Colorado border to southern New Mexico, which intuitively translates into moving a few yards a day.

—Increasing volcanic activity on Earth is spewing gold and iridium into the atmosphere—an active volcano may release one pound of gold a day into the air. Earth intelligence.

—The ark, originally taken by the Levites to Aswan in Egypt (to the island of Elephantine), was transported again approximately fifth century B.C. by descendants of the Jews to Ethiopia. When the Black Jews were airlifted out of Ethiopia in the early 1990s and transported to Israel, David asks if the ark of the Covenant went with them. (Read Graham Hancock's book, *The Sign and the Seal*.)

—Nostradamus said that the occult gold would be known to science by 1999.

—Rhodium and iridium, in their non-monatomic states, are naturally found in slippery elm bark, sheep swirl, grape seed extract, and aloe vera and carrot juice. (Iridium speeds metabolism forty percent so should not be used if there is cancer. Rhodium is the choice for cancer.)

—German biophysicist Fritz Popp has discovered that living cells emit a weak glow. He and other researchers have evidence of the coherent ordering of photons in DNA itself (from *The Quantum Self*).

—Vampires are the dark side of immortality. Vampires lose human emotion, although youth and strength are preserved by the ingestion of blood. Blood is the only "immortal" tissue in the human body; that is, there is no difference between the blood of an eighty-year-old and a twenty-year-old. Blood cells can copy themselves exactly as they renew, thus they never age. Other cells in the body make more and more imperfect copies of themselves, and thus the effects of aging.

—Other Sources: *Nexus Magazine* (Aug-Sept. '96.) "White Powder Gold: A Modern Miracle?" by David Hudson.

Chapter 19

Alien Garden

"They don't know you from Adam. And you expect to be recognized as a respected, responsible person of the world?"

—an ad of an alien gray holding an American Express Card

The mother instantly recognized certain features in the little girl, tiny with fine angel hair and pale complexion, so light, without discernible bones. The girl stood shyly behind an alien, her large, hypnotic eyes looking on like an old soul. When the alien caretakers walked the little hybrid girl away, the mother was in deep, deep sadness. The aliens, noticing this, responded by saying that she might in the future see her daughter again. Then the mother started to weep. The aliens looked surprised, as if saying, "But you are involved with it. This is a great accomplishment. Why are you so sad?"

In his book, *Secret Life*, Professor David Jacobs explores true accounts about alien-human hybrids (the aliens being the grays with large eyes). The hybrid children are not turning out as well as the aliens might have wished. The babies are listless, more sickly than human babies. In general, they do not respond like human babies. A woman said, "I carry it around. I feel as if it needs the rhythm . . . they (the aliens) can't do it . . ."[1] Aliens bring human mothers into the nurseries to watch how human mothers hold their babies, that otherwise die without human bonding.

The grays are thought to be a highly intelligent but physically deteriorating species whose gene pool is weakened, even dying. Their digestion is also atrophied, nonfunctional. They have been witnessed rubbing hydrogen peroxide on their skin to absorb the hormonal secretions obtained from the tissue extract from cows they have mutilated.[2] In mutilations, blood is removed down to the capillary level, the eyes, lower jaw, tongue, urinary tract, and rectum are often taken (maybe for testing of radiation effects). Humans have been largely ignored in terms of mutilations, but cattle and humans are very similar in ways that make both attractive to the alien grays. Humans and cattle carry a perfect match of the twenty-first pair of chromosomes, as well as matches in larger fragments of four other chromosomes. Cow hemoglobin closely matches that of human blood and can be a suitable substitute for emergency transfusions. The grays apparently pulverize hormonal secretions for the subtle essences of our biological life. Beta-carbolines are found in both human and cow urine, blood plasma and platelets, cerebral spinal fluid, the retina and pineal gland. Betacarbolines can trigger dreams and are possibly used by the alien grays. We are their garden, and they have sought the newer human gene pool to strengthen the species and even to beautify their appearance.

In his book *Communion*, Whitley Strieber asked one gray female why she looked so ugly, and she answered, "I can't help that."[3] This is odd in that most species consider their own kind the most attractive. In order to upgrade their species, the grays covertly abduct humans against their will, taking samples as if from tagged deer. They seem not terribly interested in the person's mind. The samples of ova and sperm for hybridization and incubation are taken in a clinical manner; the aim is foremost a biological one.

In August 1994, in Truchas, New Mexico there were three cattle mutilations. Two days prior to this, myself and a friend shared the same dream. We both dreamt of a young woman with dark hair and olive skin who seemed asleep, or had been put to sleep. In my dream she was presented to me by men in white, who held her, then laid her body on a table. I was compelled somehow to eat some tissue from her left breast, which I took from her and gulped down feeling repulsed. My friend's dream was the same, except that the woman was presented to her by "men in black with alien-like faces," and she also ate flesh from the woman's left face down to her breast. When my friend and I compared notes, we wondered if the dreams were of mutilation, and the woman symbolized New Mexico. My husband and I had also seen a UFO hanging in the skies those nights.

It is enigmatic that the grays, who traverse the universe in time machines, come to us to correct a genetic problem. Why not travel instead back in time and correct their own species? The paradox is that the grays have been forced unexpectedly to observe human emotion, spontaneity and free will. We can only imagine the experience of hybrids, pale, intelligent, and phlegmatic beings, born rare as whooping cranes.

ALIEN GARDEN HYBRID

The young friend she calls son
goes off in October grass
to feel the watercolor of surprise.
He is barely up against the metal sky
or the fall apples swollen in his hands

though the sickness makes him pale
mother says, You are loved the most,
dancing bee of the heart,
so sing and rest.
Sing and rest.

he goes down to meet the bee
to hum inside the grass
find his terrible happiness

she fears nature is revealing secrets
to her son, that he will flee
like beauty and pain in a fox hunt,

he already knows
heart is where a creature
places something, looks back
then enters the water

he will tell you
of his fascination
for lost worlds, for the play
of whooping cranes

he will tell you
he is already there,
and to sing to him.
Sing to him.

Many researchers say that a pact was made with the grays around WWII and after the 1947 Roswell saucer crash in New Mexico for technology in exchange for the harvest of cattle and humans, which the government thought the aliens would do anyway. Dr. Oberth, the rocket specialist in the late 1950s said, "Gentlemen, we cannot take all the credit for our civilization's rapid technical advancement over the past decade. We have had help." When questioned as to who helped us, he replied, "Those guys, out there from the other planets."[4] Consider the technology of a UFO, the ultimate physics, or the B-2 stealth bomber, or the pulse drive aircraft seen in 1994 that moved so fast no camera could capture it as it left clouds spaced like pulses. Where are the grays from?

At the time of the famous Roswell, New Mexico saucer incident, Gerald Anderson, age five, saw alien bodies at the second site—175 miles west of Roswell on the plains of San Augustin—while rockhounding with his family. An archeological group also walked onto the scene—the group having thought it saw a meteor or plane crash in that area. Gerald recalled the thirty-five foot diameter disc where it "got cooler as one neared the craft—like refrigerated air, though it was very dry and hot out there." The craft had an acetone smell. There were four bodies, two dead, one injured, and one alive. The injured one was lying on something like tin foil. Another with almond shiny eyes was looking back and forth at the sky. It never made a sound. Gerald stated that he leaned over the alive one

(Gerald himself as a child being similar in size to an alien). He said, "I could feel (the gray's) the sensation of tumbling, falling, and the loneliness of never getting back where it came from." Soon, the military arrived and hurried everyone off at gunpoint. "We were herded like cattle," said Gerald, who also observed that when the alien saw the military "it went into a panic."[5]

At the Roswell crash site "Mac" Brazel's son Bill found debris with writing like hieroglyphics, which was "embossed in appearance on the metal and had a purplish violet hue." The piece was later confiscated by the military. At the same time, KOAT radio in Albuquerque, New Mexico was told by the FBI to cease and desist, to not release the Roswell crash information. KGFL radio was told its license would be taken if information on the Roswell incident was released. Besides abridgment of Freedom of Speech, C.A.U.S.— Citizens Against UFO Secrecy—filed a writ of habeas corpus in 1994 to free any extraterrestrial beings held in captivity. I am sure hybrids are included in the spirit of this action. On the other hand, maybe it is we being held captive. Maybe aliens are at the top of secret societies.

In September 1961, while driving through the White Mountains of New Hampshire, Betty and Barney Hill were abducted by aliens. In the alien craft, Betty was shown a three-dimensional star map that showed where the grays' home is. When she had a difficult time reading it, the aliens looked disappointed. The map, she said, was a window two feet high, and four feet long that showed balls with heavy lines depicting frequently traveled routes, and the ones less traveled with dotted lines. Later, drawing the map from memory, Betty Hill gave it to Marjorie Fish, a school teacher. Marjorie Fish matched stars on Earth star maps with Betty's sketch. Noting the stars most likely to have life, Marjorie tried thousands of combinations, then found only one that matched. What she discovered was a pair of stars, Zeta 1 and Zeta 2 Reticuli, which are one billion years older than Earth in evolution.

Humankind still waits for concrete evidence that the aliens exist. Betty Hill nearly retrieved a book from an alien, but then the group decided against it. Betty did get some information that points away from 'fantasyland' in 1961, when she recalled the aliens inserting a needle into her navel, which she was told was for a pregnancy test. It was not until the 1970s that amniocentesis was developed. Antonio

Villas-Boas, a Brazilian farmer, tried to garner physical evidence for the existence of aliens when, in October 1957, an alien craft landed near his tractor. Stealing a clock-like mechanism, he unfortunately was caught, and this attempt failed too.[6] A model of the human brain was shown to a human abductee by a humanoid alien who asked the abductee where the subconscious mind is located.[7] We may associate the subconscious with an infinite frontier, but the grays view the subconscious concretely. Their own subconscious may be more limited. The grays are said to have an extra lobe in their brain. A gray may be similar to the anteater-like echidna that also has an extra lobe. (The echidna is one of the few mammals that doesn't dream.) The extra lobe may be to compensate for not dreaming, to process the extra stimuli. How sad not to dream, but to abduct, like wolves running through an invisible forest.

The grays and other aliens are thought to be hanging out around paramilitary bases, underground, or on the Martian moon Phobos—or even on the Earth's moon—and hiding out in the asteroid belt, the firmament between Jupiter and Mars. Or the aliens might be hiding in our DNA.

For abductees, the grays reside in memories at levels both psychological and physiological. This is because during any highly stressed novel event, or trauma, a numbing or psycho-physiological shock begins. One then enters an altered state of consciousness. Hormonal neuromodulators are released by the limbic, hypothalamic, pituitary, and adrenal systems and begin to affect most cells, tissues, and organ systems in the body. They encode all the internal and external impressions of the trauma during the shock state. As the person returns to a normal physiologic state, the vivid memories are not available to normal consciousness, but instead are said to be deeply imprinted on physiological memory. The memory is held in the tissues due to a physiological state. Dreams are also hard to recall because one's chemistry and brain waves alter during the waking process.

Can the gray experience be compared to a vision like a white buffalo, or an eagle? If so, where is the art, literature, and music that responds to these abductions? Throughout history, stories, fables, and art depict humans intermixing with other beings. The early pre-Christian Celts believed in the Blessed Otherworldly Islands where humans and fairies intermingled sexually. In the

Middle Ages were the succubi. With the grays, however, the stories are so much the same—dry, clinical, unaesthetic. Like the film, "Wild Palms," wherein the rhinoceros is what is left over of the magical unicorn. Or what is left of a Tibetan mandala—an unadorned gray UFO. But then, there are reports enough of abductees who speak of the grays in a deeply stirring way. A few researchers have stated that the grays are simply shaved rhesus monkeys employed by the secret government. But do rhesus monkeys walk upright, have deep, soulful eyes, and speak telepathically? There may be a message we are missing.

When we are ready, the universe approaches in power and ecstasy. If we are not ready, the universe tears us asunder. *The Black Cloud*, a 1957 film by Fred Hoyle, discussed by Jung in his book, *Flying Saucers*, is about a black cloud that moves toward our solar system, feeding on our sun.[8] Perceiving it as a threat, earthlings fire at it with H-bombs. When that fails, it is decided to communicate with it. Those on Earth find that the cloud is 500 million years old. A young physicist then declares he is ready to hear the cloud's message. He gets into a hypnotic condition but then dies of a sort of inflammation of the brain. Then, out of the blue, the cloud decides to quit our solar system, the planet earth meanwhile in disarray. Jung interpreted this to mean that the earthlings had been "too immature to seize the message." The Sun loses no energy, but humans pay a great price for the irruption of the unconscious. The cloud sinks back to its former distance. It disturbs one knowing that something out there doesn't want us in the general reality. With no guideposts to go by, are we but superfluous participants, set up even for an anti-experience?

Grays have been compared to insects by humans. As with termites, the grays appear very collective in their high intelligence, which may be therefore not really intelligence, but more a strong morphogenetic field. The central brain and life source in a termite colony is its queen. A pulsating huge center, she delivers 10,000 eggs a day, her body looking like the pale hemispheres of a brain. The queen-god, who lives half a century, generates the field of space and time across which workers run their functions. Telepathic . . . or an insane psychedelia, for termite farmers even cultivate tiny mushrooms in their gardens. The mud mound, guarded by soldiers, has its greatest enemy in the sun. The sun can dry the mound to dust. An underground society, there is probably no crime inside the mound. All is harmonious, collective, and useful. The queen, great beast, focuses all on her unselfish purpose. Emotions do not get out of hand. No termite face can even express this.

We humans "aligned with God" are so imperfect by comparison. Seeking an individual purpose, causing havoc. The insects adapt to survive. In Genesis, humanity is to learn how to dominate a place we are only partly from, because it is easily taken back by the insects. In terms of hybrids, are we to be the pupa of another species? Will we recognize ourselves, or forget as does the butterfly that it was once a caterpillar, utterly different in body and function? Will the human side of hybrids suddenly go hyperdimensional, like the insects which learned to fly the sky fifty million years before any other creature? Will this all come to some higher purpose? Will hybrids see a universe humans will only dream of fifty million years from now? Or will they miss the view, like mayflies that are born, mate and die in a single day? Too bad mayflies don't hatch on Venus, where a day is longer than a year, where the mayfly could mate in four seasons.

The grays may have emerged at their appointed time, like moles in the universe, for us to wrestle with. As Will is that seed planted in us to go to God freely, the grays seem to set us up for an anti-experience. They are not evil, but they are not good. They write on us as slate, with probes and implants. They repossess our seed. It feels like a power failure. A fallen star. For their paradise is black and white, while ours is new and beautiful, a glorious knock.

DISTURBANCES IN BLACK AND WHITE

This being . . . what is she crying for?
but that was already anticipated
a power failure
(We have waited a long time for this.)
nothing
and the world arrives
the great repossession
inventories of moles and squirrels
that grow into a glorious knock
in the black and white paradise

a great harvest of eggs
and other mates
dark probes that move like injured Will
over the blue and gray chalkboards
because that was its only food
You had better get a Moses,
and a god-box
for the orphan inside you
the serpent, and feed them
love; do not recoil
and they will remember
to dream that night.

The grays as our destiny. A future that is a gray disc. Do not accept it. The human past has been more beautiful than that—and another future will arrive.

A Celebese tribe says it literally descended from sky ships from the stars. But these ancestors were not the grays. It is said that their king's first ancestor descended from the Pleiades. The King's house, like others of the tribe, is built like an ark-ship. Tribe genealogy can be traced back to the Pleiades where beings peaceful and free reside. An elderly Balinese man, an artist known for his temple architecture, met the astronaut Ron Evans, who walked on the Moon. Both claim to have been on the Moon. The astronaut arrived in a physical capsule, the Balinese tribal artist arrived in the place of psyche—which is more real?

Humans have the innate subconscious talent for projecting their own "destiny" out in the world, which gives the outside object a numinosity that it is doing something to us, or relating to us. The unconscious also enlivens, and we meet somewhere in the imaginary space between ourselves and the object. Feelings like merging, peace, beauty, power, and deep meaning have been associated with monoliths, the Moon, rainbows, strangers, and UFOs. Human nature attaches itself to both living and non-living objects. This is what humans have that the grays have yet to demonstrate to us.

Notes:

—If the grays time-traveled to their past in order to correct their DNA, all that would happen in quantum physics is that they could wormhole into a new, improved parallel universe. However, the original past would still remain as well (the past remains the past) in some universe, being one of the manifested probable timelines.

"Soon, the gate will open and she will walk into her position in His place, and eat the grass He places before her. While she eats, He will relieve the pain until morning. After that, the Man will walk away with white water in a round container. The Guernsey does not know where he got the white water nor why He desires it."[9]

—on "Loosh," from Far Journeys, Robert Monroe

Loosh

In the quiet Iowa town, a woman watches from her room feeling somewhat absent. The falling blossoms have what she has not—a brief brilliance that strikes the earth. This thought arose earlier that day while she was milking the family cow, a black and white Guernsey with eyes of velvet sleep. The loosh spilled like blossoms, the cow munching, oblivious to what it was producing. As she toted the pails back to the clapboard house, the thought occurred that perhaps she was no different from the cow! She too was producing something of value of which she was oblivious. She knew it must be something natural in her, caught in the gentle hands of the earth. But her instinct was to feel superior to the cow. After all, she was a more graceful creature, a more conscious being! Yet, back in her familiar kitchen, while storing the loosh in bottles, minus a warm glass for herself, she did acknowledge "It is the near perfect food." She reflected that this milk was even more pure than the commercial milk sold in cartons, with the pictures of missing children. She then recalled the mild mannered Guernseys, like huge black and white flowers from which she gathered. She made a promise then and there to produce, produce, produce! And she felt this almost romantically, as if she were a poet dying of consumption (by now she had a white mustache). But what was it she was producing? And sleep comes over her. The milk cow is down on her knees, the sun is crouching in the trees. The black sky whirls meteors—each one falls as if on a passionate sword. Her mind spills loosh . . . Loosh.

Chapter 20

Cetacean Garden

Species of Baleen Whales	Species of Toothed Whales
Blue	Sperm
Sperm	Beaked
Right	Killer/Orca
Humped	Dolphin

"For as Jonas was three days and three nights in the whale's belly; so shall the Son of man be three days and three nights in the heart of the earth."

—Jesus' answer to those seeking a sign, Matthew (12:39-40)

*E*volution suggests that whales and dolphins were once land mammals, and hoofed. Legend has it that dolphins were once in the form of humans but returned again to the sea. Indeed, there are humans that yearn to enter the sea and join a pod of dolphins. And humans, having such smooth skin, are well suited for the water.

I had a friend who went to Las Vegas, Nevada. She soon tired of gambling casinos, and instead decided to visit the dolphin tank at the Mirage Hotel, which is owned by the musician Michael Jackson. As she was standing by the tank, a dolphin swam by and began to roll and play near her. She felt strongly compelled to dive into the tank. Minutes later, security pulled her out.

Dolphins have long been associated with humanity's psyche. Apollo's temple at Delphi has sculpted dolphins, the word Delphi being derived from delphys meaning womb, and delphis meaning dolphin. Are we pupae from dolphins? In Hinduism, Shrimad Bhagavatum, the heavens, are said to represent the shape of a dolphin. Do we return to the dolphin?

Dolphins are born happy, and arc in happiness from the womb into the ocean. The only enemy of the dolphin is the shark, and humankind. Overall, dolphins are loved around the world, though they are sacrificed to tuna nets. In ancient Greece it was considered murder to slay a dolphin.

Bottle-nosed dolphins have over 1500 grams more associative brain mass than humans. The dolphin brain is thirty million years ahead of ours in evolutionary development. The size-ratio of a dolphin's cortex to its limbic system is greater than in most humans. These creatures manifest high intelligence without tools. The cetaceans, dolphins and whales, are like yogis because they "breathe" spherically, bringing the prana life force through the top of the head and also up through the perineum. (This spherical breathing is like a Mer Ka Ba meditation.) For yogis, spherical breathing opens the pineal gland, which is the seat of the soul and a center of bliss. Early humans "breathed" this life force through the soft part of the cranium, which now calcifies around the age of a year and a half. One can feel the sacral-cranial pulsations, especially on an infant.

The Dogon tribe of Africa, near Timbuktu, say that from the star Sirius came dolphin-like beings, amphibious humans that communicated secrets and sang like sirens to them. What lends so much credence to this story is that the Dogon high priests knew about the tiny star Sirius B which orbits Sirius A even before it was seen by moderns in 1970 via a telescope launched in space. Sirius B, a white dwarf, is invisible to the eye, but the Dogon tribe was even able to discuss its orbit and knew it was made of the heaviest matter in the universe. These dolphin-people arrived in a flying saucer.

John Lilly, an American neurophysiologist known for his work with dolphins, said in a lecture, he was "overwhelmed by the huge dolphin mind," when he entered it while in an isolation tank. He emphasized that it was a benevolent mind, but so vast it "overwhelmed" him.

Dolphins are individual and yet move as "One Mind and One Body."[1] Dolphins enter an altered state as a pod in the evenings just before sundown. Then the dolphins swim out of the bays to join larger pods. Each dolphin remains an individual, however, as the pods grow larger, more illumined. Dolphins live in at least the illumined mind, as demonstrated by their sense of joy, play, and love of freedom. Many humans feel, especially in water, an instant sense of peace and well-being near a dolphin. Dolphins emit sounds and pulses in a frequency that stimulates the release of endorphins in the human brain. This presence of dolphin consciousness increases one's sense of joy.

Being in the company of dolphins enhances learning and healing. The immune system is bolstered. At the Dolphin Center in the Florida Keys, disabled kids swim with dolphins and many speak their first words up to ten times faster than with conventional therapy.[2] Autistic children even peek out from their shells.

Dr. John Lilly insists that a bottle-nosed dolphin has learned to speak English, "albeit with a strong Hungarian accent." The dolphin apparently learned from Dr. Kert, a Hungarian-born physicist who led a research team at Marine World in Redwood City, California, in the 1980s.

Dolphins enter a one mind place, but not as captives. Only dolphins in captivity will attack a human. Trainers have admitted sadly that to teach a captured dolphin to perform, it must be dominated, kept hungry, hit with pool brushes, and wrapped in spook nets. The Dolphin Research Center on Grassy Key is well known for its rehabilitation of sick, wounded show dolphins. It is a refuge for burnt-out show dolphins and those frazzled from crowded facilities.

Somehow she is drowning
the salt sighs a little
like skin and veins
her eyes have netted the tragic light
sunset, an erosion of sky

but the pink coral at dusk
is luminous
and reproaches extinction

Dolphins have long been used by the Navy as runners of explosives. Recently, in the winter of 1994, dolphins Jake, Luther, and Buck won the first "Navy Discharge" of any dolphins in history. They were released from San Diego to Sugarloaf Dolphin Sanctuary on Sugarloaf Key. Rick O'Barry, former Flipper trainer turned anti-captivity activist, went to San Diego and rode back with the dolphins to Florida. He wanted them released back to the Gulf of Mexico where they were captured in 1989 (when the Berlin Wall fell) but they have not received federal permission yet.

Arabic tradition says the earth rests on the back of a whale. The blue whale is the best suited mammal for this, being the largest animal ever on the earth, weighing up to 220 tons and having a length of one hundred feet.

Whales have a brain seven times the size of ours, but the whale's brain size to body mass ratio is still small relative to the ratio of a human's brain to its human body mass. But then, the brain to mass ratio of a human is actually smaller than the ratio of a marmoset's brain is to its body mass! Thus we are left with Melville's dilemma in the novel, *Moby Dick*, as to whether the whale was a genius, or a simple brute. In any case, whales are the succesors of carnivorous mammals that returned to the sea fifty to seventy million years ago. Placid browsers, they dive the deeps like a sublime meditation. The whale's heartbeat may slow to four beats a minute on a dive to depths of—for the sperm whale—3300 feet and more and at a pressure of 100 atmospheres. Here, the whale sounds where exotic life in the abyss resides, its blood, the multitudinous speech. Here, the sperm whale is perhaps the only creature to have seen a live and well giant squid, architecteuteuthis, which lives 1000 meters under the sea. We humans see this creature of myth that strangles whole ships of sailors only when it is sickly and washed ashore, or else in the stomach of a sperm whale. None have been maintained in aquariums. Most highly intelligent of the invertebrates, this cephalopod, "head-foot", has reached physical dimensions of sixty feet and weighed a ton. Its motor neurons have been examined by scientists to calculate the velocity of neurons, the dark iris of its huge eye, mirroring the deep aboriginal abyss.

Like aborigines who uphold the world by singing the songlines, so do the whale songs uphold the world. Whales have been singing for fifty to sixty million years, repeating their songs like a Homer telling the *Odyssey*, an oral tradition. There are whale songs with a similar length of "notes and stanzas" as found in the content of the *Iliad* and *Odyssey*. Songs are exact, the way aboriginal Australian songs are rulers that measure and keep the earth in resonance. A whale may leave winter waters in the middle of a song and return months later and continue at the right note, although humpbacks may improvise like a jazz theme. In theory, the reflective surfaces of the entire Earth (25,000 miles in circumference) can be sounded by a whale. Whale songs already breadth the Pacific Ocean. A whale song haunts the blue moaning north.

Humpback and sperm whales have held "conversations" with sounding devices of ships. Too much noise pollution can confuse, even if of natural causes. In June 1979, forty-one sperm whales beached on the Oregon coast at Florence. The whales were lost because they were not getting back the same echoes they were sending out. The episode was followed by four earthquakes at Big Bear, California. Perhaps the whale's sonar was jammed by the approaching quakes.

A whale or great fish, also beached in the form of a crop circle at Lockeridge, Wilts in Britain. It was a fish-like shape with fins and rings around the head and tail, as if schools of tiny fish had in a minute dance swirled the field into whale.

The octopus merits some adoration—a cephalopod, a huge head on a foot, not quite a cetacean, but extremely intelligent. An invertebrate which lives a mere two to three years, so vulnerable, like humans, that it has had to use its brains to survive. In a Jacques Cousteau film, an octopus learned to uncork a glass jar which held a lobster inside. This was the first time in octopi history that a lobster in a glass jar was presented to an octopus. The octopus actually "sat" back to cerebrate, its arms wrapped around its head. Then, with one quick motion, it unscrewed the cork and won the prize—a lobster.

My husband Marc knew of a baby octopus at Sea Camp in Big Pine Key Florida that learned what time of day the door to its aquarium opened. One day, the octopus slipped through the aquarium door out of the lab, over coral where it lost an arm, and back to the sea. An ancient mollusk, a cephalopod, head on foot, the octopus walks though the surf with its high intelligence. It has nearly human eyes. One female octopus bonded with a scuba diving man. She reached out to pull him closer to her by his mask.

Notes:

—Humans and cetaceans share characteristics of neotony, which designates a kind of arrested development in evolution wherein a certain immature, even embryonic characteristic remains in mature individuals—like the love of playing.

—Cetaceans may have holographic brains/minds. Holograms have been constructed from sound waves. Large whales and dolphins have more gray matter than humans.

—Dolphins have a highly extensive cortex, but it is much thinner than a human's. However, the size-ratio of a dolphin cortex to its limbic system is greater than in most humans. Dolphins are born with fifty percent of their adult brain size, while humans are born with twenty-five percent of the full adult brain size.

—A re-birther under Stanislov Grof painted an octopus in the womb, tentacles free and afloat like a meaningless neuron, frightening as they can seemingly attach to anything—like free-floating anxiety.

—The Dogon of Mali, Africa, speak of their roots in Egypt, and of encountering dolphin-like beings who arrived in a UFO. These beings taught the Dogon's ancestors about the binary star system, Sirius B and A, and of astronomy and geometry. Ancient Egypt had a brief dynasty wherein Sirians ruled, immortals from Sirius who were gentle, truthful, and psychic by nature. These beings were ten to fifteen feet tall with huge backward sloping heads, huge ears, long necks, wide mermaid hips, smooth skin, and often appeared naked. Statues, busts, and paintings depicting these physical characteristics may be seen in the Egypt of Pharaoh Akhenaten and Nefertiti of the eighteenth dynasty (1355 B.C.) when the art of Egypt took a realistic bent. During this dynasty, for example, paintings of birds are more like nature and less stylized. Pharaoh Akhenaten was detested by the people because he taught that they did not need their priests, nor their many gods. He said that the one God is within. He was also a pacifist. War could only be used to protect their borders if attacked. He also initiated 300 Christ-like beings, mostly women, who were the root of the Essene brotherhood that left the Great Pyramid and migrated to Masada. Christ and Mother Mary were Essenes, immortals—and they were despised by the local priesthood. Christ is associated with the fish, whale, and in ancient script, the dolphin. (See Flower of Life Workshop videos by Drunvelo.) Curiously, in Peru, the Incans tried to elongate infant heads to mimic the gods.

—The unicorn may be the magical ancestor of the whales. One night while working at the hospital, I met a registered nurse, Denys Cope, who told me of a childhood memory. The memory, or rather deep knowing inside her, was that "The unicorn realized, as the Ark sailed past, that a flood was coming, and in order to survive, all the unicorns would have to evoke their magic to become sea creatures." Decades after her childhood vision, Denys found a greeting card that pictured two unicorns standing on the shore as the Ark sailed away. It is known that the whale was once a land mammal and hoofed. Denys later learned that the horn of the narwhal was sold as the horn of the unicorn during the Renaissance to make cups that were said to detoxify any poisonous drink.

It Is Not Certain That Whales Pray

It is not certain that whales pray. They do provide oil, fragrances, and their body to eat (although a plate of whale seems at first profane compared to a delicate host). Whales are sacred in the gifts they bear, and are sometimes compared with Christ. But they do not resurrect, something quite different from "He rises!," nor do they confer unmerited grace. But the extraordinary thing about these most massive of creatures is that they produce the least massive of earthly things—light. One may read about the whale by its own light, that is, by oil lamp. Now if whales could learn to read by their own light, that would be divine. Whales then could be likened to the thirteenth century Tibetan monks who could read in the dark by the light given off by their own bodies! But the oil of whales is only gotten after the mammal has succumbed to whale hunters, and a dead whale is not inspiring to our modern readers who have electricity.

And "who" is this unctuous being, its crown wrapped with the purest burning oil? Is it any wonder hunters have sought it, and for more than its flesh? Whales have enchanted many a naturalist, adventurer, and artist. Few great works have been inspired by species like squirrels or cows (with the exception of my piece on Guernseys, entitled "Loosh"). For the avid whale watcher, there is charm even in the whale's tail. Unlike other tails, which are inferior in that they wiggle, reminding us of an earlier evolutionary time, the whale's tail is horizontal, and waves aesthetically. Moreover, no one disputes that it is a powerful tail, and has been used as a weapon. Adult male whales have been witnessed to rush each other viciously at great speed. What of the whale's color? Moby Dick's whiteness has provoked the imagination of many critics. It has been suggested that his whiteness is the color of resurrection or annihilation, of purity or deformity. But I ask, could the whale be like an albino, essentially normal, but embarrassed by sun?

The Splash Between Them

After a day pounding the pavement she exclaims, "I can't work in a factory!" and it was Monday again, all you can eat jumbo shrimp at the C-side Cafe. Her beau, Seymour, once said, "You know, kid, all things have their place, out at sea. I always remember that, if a fish wanders from its normal depth, it risks falling." She wished he were here now! Not away on that government research grant, clocking dolphins up to twenty-five miles an hour! Seymour, among waves clothed in thunder, captured her. And it was Seymour, at Sea World, who incited a referendum in favor of moving the dolphin tank out of sight of the shark cage, shouting with sustained emotion, "Sharks eat dolphins!"

Once at sea, she was able to be the voice and strength behind Seymour. She'd even dreamt of a honeymoon in the Virgin Islands watching the dolphins. She and Seymour sipping pina colada under an umbrella, a band playing, jazz notes clipping across the sand. Above them, clarinet sun.

But her reverie was broken when she saw that Seymour had gotten sick, holding pathetically to the railing, the doctor shaking his head, "No, it can't be," while she insisted, "I'm telling you it's in the tuna salad, there's dolphin in that tuna." The doc later called her "perversely willful."

The boat docked at the nearest port. She felt like an ant nudged up a blade of grass, as if up a plank, a bag in each of her hands, Seymour blew her a kiss saying, "Remember there's a place for you!" the last splash between them.

She was, in the end, rational, self-sufficient. Not for her to wax and wane on some melancholic shore, in eternal cold! On nice days she could be found sketching on the beach. Sometimes a little sand was teasingly kicked her way; she would glance up at the wet bronze legs, the Hollywood smile with bright quick dimples, before returning to her sketch pad. And what was she sketching? Not the local fauna! What captured her fancy was a tome of long-extinct creatures. (Did Seymour somehow trigger this sentiment?) It was the late Cretaceous period that hooked her. Known by the birth of flowering plants, and the death of dinosaurs, it seemed metaphoric of her own inner metamorphosis. Around the margins of her notepad she penciled in slender crinoids, reptile-like plants with scaly leaves. Her mind dreamed Animalia, numinous bottom dwellers like she imagined her own deep psyche to be! And then the trilobites! Rising up like the first shamans, they were the first Animalia to possess vision. With up to 750 lenses, they stared, frozen-jointed, limbs on a segmented body, now dyed impressions on rock, still looking over the primordial ooze. Finally, they molted, a rebirth! she read, leafing on the sand.

Though it was a reprieve to ponder extinction, and fathomless depths of time, the old guilt, for not procuring a job, resurfaced. She told herself the right job would eventually find her. She would have to wait, simply endure it. And she mused about jobs one could do at home—that wouldn't crimp her style—like sewing buttons for eyes on stuffed cats via mail order.

And on these sensitive days even a puff of sand blown her way elicited not a smile, but a hurt in her eyes, and she would wrestle all day with questions like "What did he mean by that?" "What's wrong with me!" she'd silently cry, for even her sketches of trilobites seemed to turn against her. Inevitably, she could be found in bed, the clock hands not moving at all. Yet, like the oceans ebb and rise, she was soon back on the beach, vigorously sketching. It was on one of these happier days, pulling crumbly shrimp from her bag, that an elderly man came her way, scuffing up a little sand. His hobby, he said, was anthropology. Soon they were in a frolicsome argument about *The Origin of Species*, and the nostalgia of water. She asked, "So where did we come from . . . so suddenly, I mean . . . Do you believe in UFO's?" For a second his body shook like a spasm, then he froze, staring at her. "Man is king! We're it, young lady, and don't you forget it!" He then rattled down the shore, his limbs almost disjointed, reminding her of something.

She presses her feet into the sand. She slides into the water. She wraps herself in a peach-colored wave.

Chapter 21

Impostors

"Countless dark bodies are to be inferred near the sun."

—Nietzsche, Beyond Good and Evil

*H*e is now about fourteen years old, going on fifteen. He is the singular citizen of no nation, yet is granted citizenship to all nations. His super-elite family, inner circle, and staff maintain homes all over the world. He has learned to speak many languages, including obscure and ancient dialects.

In June 1992, *Newsweek* had an article with the headline, "The Future Is Here," with the focus on the ecological summit at Rio De Janeiro. A large color ad focused on how the world environment is tied to the population of the world, and illustrated children of different nationalities beneath the headings of "North America," "South America," "Europe," "Asia," "Australia," and "Africa." The child under the "North America" heading had intelligent blue-gray eyes, set wide apart, and wavy red hair. I also noticed that the little finger on his left hand was partly missing, barely to the first knuckle. (Missing fingers often denote a genetic defect.) I was struck by this redheaded boy because he fit the physical description of a child who will come into prominence in the future as forecast by an underground writer in April, 1992.

He is not the antichrist, but the impostor child who leads the world into the New World Order Supergovernment. Recall Isaiah (11:6): "The wolf shall with the lamb also dwell . . . and a little child shall lead them." The inner child should lead us, not a celebrity of the media. What an inversion, that adults follow a media child because they are so lost. The underground writer suggested that if one looked at this young man from one angle, his features are strikingly handsome, but from another view he appears distorted or unnatural in some way. Conceived somewhere on the East Coast of the United States with fourteen other males as clones, he waits in the wings to be presented at the appropriate hour in world events. A prodigy in music, literature, world philosophy and intercultural aspects of religions worldwide, ecological and environmental, he will be, the writer warns: "replete with apparently perfect solutions to the nightmare conditions prevailing in the world." He will be able to expound on traditional scriptures, New Age thought, Eastern traditions, Muslim doctrine, Buddhist thought. As New World Order companies and corporations support and promote him, many will fall under the spell. Any who question him will be pressured to retract, so voracious will be the hunger for innocence and solutions. Although he will speak a beautiful universal language, will this really be love, or entrapment? And why red hair? Perhaps because the color red is charged with emotion.

There has been an attempt at world citizenship, which I discovered at the House of Common Law at the Santa Fe township: world citizen Davis v. District Director, Immigration, et cetera. Gary Davis, plaintiff on May 25, 1948, a bomber pilot in World War II, recorded:

> I desire to make a formal renunciation of my American nationality . . . I no longer find it compatible with my inner conviction . . . by remaining solely loyal to one of these sovereign nation-states . . . I should like to consider myself a citizen of the world."

On May, 1977, the petitioner attempted to enter the United States on a passport issued by the "World Service Authority," an organization promoting world citizenship. Petition was denied. "The court in no way wishes to deprecate the honesty of belief or depth of conviction that the petitioner feels for the cause of world citizenship."[1]

World Citizenship is being planned, however, and below is an excerpt of a preliminary draft of a World Constitution:

> The people of the world have agreed that the advancement of man in spiritual excellence and physical welfare is the common good of mankind . . . the age of nations must end . . . to which they surrender their arms . . . to establish this Constitution as the covenant and fundamental law of the Federal Republic of the World . . . The principles underlying the Rights of man are and shall be permanently stated in the Duty of everyone everywhere, whether a citizen sharing in the responsibilities and privileges of World Government or a ward and pupil of the World Commonwealth: to serve the . . . common cause . . . to abstain from violence except for repulse of violence as commanded or granted under law. Social duty (is) protection of individuals and groups against subjugation and tyrannical rule. The four elements— earth, water, air, energy—are the common property of the human race. The administration of the world bank and the establishment of suitable world fiscal agencies for the issue of money and creation and control of credit . . . the establishment, regulation, and when necessary or desirable the operation of means of transportation and communication which are of federal interest. The supervision and approval of laws concerning emigration and immigration and the movements of peoples, the appropriation, under the right of eminent domain, of such private or public property as may be necessary for federal use, reasonable compensation being made thereof . . .

Within the first three years of world government the council and the president shall establish three special bodies, namely:

a) The house of nationalities and states, with representatives from each, for the safeguarding of local institutions and autonomies and the protection of minorities.

b) a syndical or functional senate, for the representation of syndicates and unions or occupational associations and any other corporate interests of transnational significance,[1] as for mediation or arbitration in non-justifiable issues among such syndicates or unions or other corporate interests.

c) an institute of science, education, and culture.[2]

The above constitution is in the hands of a few powerful groups with no checks and balances. There are no individual unalienable rights. The goal is a federal corporation, a military-corporate socialist state. The United Nations is a major arm in this. (The United Nations is not a corporation, but was chartered in 1945. It is based on treaties. The United States won its independence via a treaty.) In June 1982, in a special session on disarmament, the United Nations denied freedom of speech to Hopi elders, who since the 1960s have warned of the end of this world by fire if humankind continues to live in disharmony with nature. The Hopi elders did submit written proposals to the United Nations body.

The United Nations hopes to end wars and brutality, famine, and pestilence that have been the Old World Order. The peace and order that follow the end of war, hunger, and personal property is a delightful, almost Christ-like idea. However, the individual can become squelched in bureaucracy and corporate law and monies, and be devoid of inalienable rights for the "greater society."

I have heard that Washington, D.C. is establishing itself as the State of New Columbia, complete with a new constitution, established when 115,000 "electors" went to the polls in 1982. Who are these anonymous creators of a new constitution? Are we being invaded? The vulture adds its shade to the tree.

Common-law counselor Jeffrey Thayer was interviewed about the State of New Columbia.[3] Mr. Thayer, whom I have talked with personally, is concerned that the local, municipal laws of the State of New Columbia will spread to the fifty states—as has federal law attempted to supercede state's rights. That is, through this constitution, citizens of the United States will not have inalienable rights—but instead civil rights, and will be defined as "clients," "customers," and "shareholders" in corporate and privatized governments. (Already, U.S. citizens have become "subjects" of Washington, D.C., the federal government, versus being sovereign over their government.) The preamble to the State of New Columbia constitution begins: "We, the people of the free and sovereign State of New Columbia, seek to secure and provide for each person: health, safety and welfare; a peaceful and orderly life; and the right to legal, social, and economic justice and equality." Thayer points out that it is the state that is sovereign here and not the people themselves—an inversion of our original Constitution and Declaration of Independence.[4]

The State of New Columbia "Bill of Rights" states:

> People with disabilities shall have the right to be treated as equal community members and the right to services AS DEFINED BY LAW in a way that promotes dignity and independence and full community participation.
>
> Youth and senior citizens have the right to enjoyment of heath and well-being as to services AS PROVIDED BY LAW NECESSARY for their development and welfare.

Phrases such as "provided by law" are about civil rights and not birthrights granted by a creator. Civil rights may change, dependent on the whims of lawmakers. One freely exercises unalienable rights, which are the ten amendments of the Bill of Rights in the 1787 Constitution. The law of this land never precluded giving dignity and care to those of the community; it is a matter of conscience. To socialize these ideas may work in small, mature communities like Denmark or Sweden. In Sweden, where health care is a social right, welfare as a generational lifestyle is very limited. Adults and parents can afford to work and not lose everything if ill or in an accident, which is not a crime.

Thayer says, "The New Columbia constitution acknowledges no higher right of privacy than one granted by the drafters themselves, pretending to be the sole source of human rights. Worse, it does not provide for unalienable rights to life, liberty or self-defense, or to acquire, hold and protect property 'free from hindrances like licenses and taxes.' There is no true free enterprise, nor true competition or recourse."

The State of New Columbia is one of the three superstates; London and the Vatican are the other two. The United States is not, however, New Columbia. The United States is a member of the United Nations. Non-members of the United Nations are: 1) The State of New Columbia, 2) the city of London, one-mile square as distinct from the United Kingdom, and 3) the Papal City, as distinct from Italy. New Columbia is subject to its own laws, but its shadow drafters may not be subject to any law—analogous to the situation wherein citizens must carry identification, unlike the "shadow government" which operates from outside any particular country, like an unmarked black helicopter.

In June 1995 I met with the author of *Conversations with Nostradamus*, Dolores Cannon, who has inadvertently encountered the prophet Nostradamus while doing hypnotic past-life regressions.[5] Thus, she has been able to make sense of his quatrains. Nostradamus was able in trance to tap into the Akashic Records (the memory of all events on earth) and he wrote in a kind of code, as the Inquisition was raging about him. Dolores Cannon has been able to decode his quatrains because the master is speaking through modern channels. Others who have tried to decipher his warnings have been able to do so only after events have taken place. (What is odd, however, is that Nostradamus insists he is still alive, and still in the 1500s!)

The incarnation of the shadow of the world is called the antichrist (not the impostor child). Nostradamus states that the antichrist was born in February 1962 and raised by a hate-filled uncle named Imam, after the antichrist's parents were killed in an Israeli conflict. In 1986 and 1987 the antichrist attended college, taking classes in computer science, economics and philosophy. The young man will lean toward want of power, but will do so with a charmingly disarming manner. So far he has remained behind the scenes, moving from location to location, meeting with an inner circle of powerful corporate leaders and financiers. This small cabal meets in a Mideast desert and eagerly supports the young man, whose precociousness and affectionate nature attracts them. The young antichrist is warmly beguiling, with a magnetic light that automatically draws one's eyes to him. He is at first a humanitarian and eventually is even considered for the Nobel Peace Prize, for nations stop making war and financial aid is sent out to those in need. Later, his humanitarianism turns into intolerance for "undesirables" and he begins campaigns to eliminate anyone who is not deemed useful to society. He has enormous power via the great communications network, which he, himself, has helped to set up.

His physical description is that of a slight build, about five feet 10 inches tall, with dark eyes, black eyebrows, and skin fairer than usual for someone living in the Mideast. (He may be out of the sun a lot.) He is casual in walk and dress, wearing tailored suits, though he tends to slouch a little. Though attractive and even handsome, the proportions of his face are off a bit. It is as if an inch of his jaw is missing. (The shape of the lower jaw has been shown to be the major abnormality in mice cultivated from frozen embryos.)[6] He wears a ring on his little finger of his left hand—yellow gold with a kind of red stone with gold fitted on top.

It is when uncle Imam dies that the antichrist comes more into power, and his true insanity, that of the inner circle, begins to manifest. Insatiable for power over the world, the antichrist becomes more and more extreme. At one point, he destroys the cultural centers of Greece and Rome. Perhaps he detests the art and beauty of these places, which are an expression of divinity in humankind. His actions paralyze the world for a while, like a cobra mesmerizing and binding its prey. Wanting no competition, he also manages to deceive a pope, and thereby unleashes secrets locked away at the Vatican Library to the entire world. This creates much dissension in the church. It is ironic here, however, that the antichrist actually works for spirit in this case, because hidden knowledge and truths are given to the world. The antichrist is an impostor mostly because he attempts to take the place of a Christ-like being. At first he presents himself in a role that is the solution to worldwide chaos. But, unlike a divine being whose light serves others, he is jealous—wanting all the world to serve him, and to satiate the bottomless pit of his hate. He becomes Satan, who always was a liar and a murderer. What is as tragic is that we, the human community of the world, align with such an impostor.

SHOOTING THE DOVE
(for John Lennon, Beatle and peacemaker, shot by a young man in 1980)

The sky falls and calls on nothing
a dove subsides; how sad the world

you are the inadequate young man
eating out of paper boxes
one bee sorting itself from the honey
out of the paper boxes

the dove flies from the branch
lost song in bending off

and Venus is too far to love
the river you want
sinks past the light that fails
if you could touch its bottom
you would be complete

your feet have already begun
left a farewell no one can name

soon you will be somebody
for shooting the dove
you imagined a heaven there

Chapter 22

Liberty

"Behold, I send you forth as sheep in the midst of wolves, be therefore wise as serpents, and harmless as doves."

—Matthew 10:16

W here Liberty is not valued, she doesn't stay. In the late 1700s, shirts, canteens, and powder horns had inscribed on them "Give me Liberty or Death." In the American Revolution, the colonists were not fighting a foreign nation, but their own government, the British Empire (although King George III is looking better all the time!), and only about three percent of the population took active part. The kingdom of God is "like a mustard seed tree," a tree that is, contrary to popular opinion, not large, being only about four feet tall—but rather, a tree hard to control, a tree hard to regulate, as is Love, Truth, Beauty, Being-ness. Also a spicy bush, the mustard seed tree can be a metaphor to spices, to the enhancement of sense. In medieval times, trade of spices helped usher in the Renaissance.

The basis of Liberty can be found in the Bill of Rights of the Constitution, and in the Declaration of Independence 1776 clause ". . . are endowed by their Creator with certain unalienable Rights, that among these are Life, Liberty, and the pursuit of Happiness." A happy nation or culture can develop a higher human nature, and harmonize more spiritually. The concept of pursuit of individual happiness, or bliss, is not found in the Communist Manifesto or the United Nations Charter.

No government can grant or take away inalienable rights, for these come from the Creator. Therefore, the main legitimate purpose of a government is to secure these rights for all its citizens. Inalienable rights apply to all human beings, regardless of religion, race, sex, or sexual preference. Inalienable rights are divine; no human has the authority to take these away from anyone.

To set the record straight, let it be known that the story of Sodom related to violent men raping angels. It was the reverse story of Genesis 6 when angels took the daughters of men as wives. This was about purity and property laws. Adultery related to property laws. If a man raped a father's daughter, the crime was to the father, not the daughter. It was fine for the father, however, to offer a daughter to a man, as when Lot offered his daughter to one of the violent men of Sodom. The Levitical law regarding "men shall not lie with men as with a woman" was written long after Moses. There were no laws against lesbianism, per se, but many laws governed heterosexual activity.

There were laws that Jews and Gentiles could not marry. The love poetry of Wisdom and Solomon is about love between stepsister and brother. There are few, if any, modern Christian marriages in the Bible.

Jesus was not traditional in his day. Jesus was treated as the son of illegitimate birth by some of his community, which would have made him an outcast. The institution of marriage was not originally related to personal love. It was the later troubadours one may thank, and they faced punishment for adultery. Jesus' emphasis was not to obey doctrine, but to follow spirit: "Man was not made for the Sabbath, but the Sabbath for Man", "When I was naked, you clothed me," and "Harlots and children will enter the kingdom first" (not born-again harlots). He was radical in treating women equally.

There is no place for domineering Pharisees in the spirit of the law. The quality of justice must be measured by one's sense of mercy. In Proverbs, Wisdom ends up in the streets, unheard by the self-righteous. Wisdom, who "sought a dwelling place among humanity, but found none," "crieth at the gates, at the entry of the city, at the coming in at the doors." Wisdom, who on earth is treated as a harlot, promises "a tree of life to those who lay hold of her" (Proverbs 9).

Civil and other rights appear in law when inalienable rights are not respected. An early license given in the U.S. was so that a black and white couple could marry.

George Mason, a Virginia planter, drafted his state's Bill of Rights—the first ten amendments which are based on inalienable rights, when we had just won our independence in 1787. At the Constitutional Convention, Thomas Jefferson sided with him. The Anabaptists at that time did not want this Bill of Rights, for they wanted a state religion (like the Catholic church became for Rome). The two beasts of Revelation are the world's controlling political and religious forces, and they put people into the "second death" of shaming, blaming, and over-burdening, in a spirit loathsome to Christ consciousness (from a lecture by Aramaic scholar, Dr. Rocco Errico of Noohra Foundation). So important is separation of church and state that a devout Jesuit said on national radio that even the choice of abortion must be fully separate from the state in order to remain a moral issue. He also commented that Jesus must have "abhorred the politicking of priests in his day—he was murdered by them."

The signers of the Declaration of Independence in 1776 and the Constitution of the United States, in 1787, were comprised of Christians, Deists, and Free Masons. It is amusing to watch fundamentalist Christians accuse Free Masons, especially the Illuminati, of usurping the Constitution, since it was written mostly by Free Masons. I attended a lecture by an ex-navy intelligence man who thought most wars were at least manipulated by, if not orchestrated by, the Brotherhood: "The Free Masons, those at the top, are the agitators of situations like Bosnia," he said. Then, at a Scottish Rite tour I overheard two brothers say, "If only there was more of the Brotherhood, we wouldn't have the Bosnias of the world." Free Masons helped Pierre L'Enfant design Washington, D.C., to be geometrically in coherence with the earth grid. This was so that emotion and perception could be radiated coherently throughout the land. Ironically, Pierre was eventually fired due to his perfectionistic nature.

Our founders were somewhat opposed to each other. The Jeffersonians wanted a firm constitutional republic, a limited government. The Hamilton federalists wanted chartered banks and corporations, and stronger armed forces. Hamilton invented the concept of "implied powers," which in the modern world of contracts means "implied consent," wherein one hands authority over to a third party. Under Jefferson, individuals would thrive in a peaceful agrarian culture. (But then, such states often end up being run by foreign powers with strong armies and resourceful banks.)

Democracies are not always geared toward individual liberties, nor individual excellence. In an unlimited democracy, one becomes all too dependent on the will of the people. Democracy tends to majority rule, which tends toward special interest groups which stampede over the individual, who is sacrificed. In our constitutional republic, one has inalienable rights, even if a majority, a "consensus" or an "opinion poll," wishes to limit, infringe or negate those rights. In a democracy one is dependent on the government for civil rights which may be granted or taken away. Our constitutional republic tends toward an anarchy where the government fears the individual will limit it. Unlimited democracies can tend toward fascism where the individual is squelched.

Ours is a history of confiscation. Sadly, immediately after we established ourselves as free of Britain, we turned around and continued to confiscate from the native Americans, the land, blacks, Mexicans in the Mexican War, Asians, women, homosexuals, Irish Catholics, many of the unborn, and other sentient beings. (To their credit, white men enacted legal recognition of inalienable rights. Many of these men were imprisoned and penniless for this conviction.) But perhaps we are longing for a history that never was. We once carried on our bodies gold coins—coins that had Lady Liberty and the eagle etched on them. These coins "rang true" when struck. This is good alchemy. But in 1933, Franklin Delano Roosevelt issued an order that it was "against public policy" for people to use gold in trade (the people were hungry and society gave no relief), so ninety-five percent of the citizens turned in their gold.

In 1934, gold certificates that were once redeemable in gold fully and immediately were also taken back by the Feds, as there wasn't enough gold for all the certificates and notes outstanding. Until 1963, currency bore a promise to pay so much "in lawful money" to the bearer on demand. In 1964, the U.S. Treasury stopped issuing silver certificates or redeemable notes. (The John F. Kennedy assassination may have been in part about having an independent accounting of the Federal Reserve. Shortly before his assassination, Kennedy issued Executive Order #11110, which would have begun abolishment of the Fed. President Johnson quickly reversed this order.) Silver coins were replaced with copper clad with silver. Dollar bills became Federal Reserve notes of debt in 1964. In 1965, the public was told by the government that silver was "too expensive" to use as money. Interestingly, one ounce of gold can buy a quality man's suit at any point in history.

Credit cards became fashionable in the 1970s, and they are now sometimes even necessary for identification and economic power. Not long ago it was socially unacceptable to hold a credit card and have debts. But few can afford to live without debt these days—being pressured to give unto Caesar what is Caesar's.

Although poverty and ailing banks are not new, somehow our substance has been eaten. From credit cards to identification cards to health cards, to Smart cards to no cards. A cashless society. Why not? One can't eat gold, and the modern person in debt does often have more possessions, as long as the rug isn't pulled out from under one. Also, in 1935, the United States possessed nearly two-thirds of all the gold in the world, yet it had the greatest number of unemployed. And it is easier to live with credit available, carrying paper money and securities. It is all based on trust. Gold is so heavy a metal—conspicuous and inconvenient. Someone could steal it from you.

Two of the major causes of the American Revolution were attempts at confiscating from the people. The Stamp Act of 1765 was a tax for the privilege of conducting a transaction in the king's domain. Like today, most transactions resulted in a tax; in 1765 it was to the king of England. The attempt to disarm militias at Concord and Lexington by the British in 1774 and 1775, and citizens being forced to quarter troops, also created great dissension. The British had become a kind of standing army and would not leave after the Indian Wars (the French and Indian Wars, 1755, between England and France prior to the American Revolution) were over.

The following is a summary of ways to confiscate rights from the individual. It could be called the Manifestation of Unchecked Democracy, or the New Federal Corporate Military State:

1) Abolition of private property:

In 1992 alone, there were 500,000 confiscations in the U.S. by the IRS—and no due process. The IRS is a private corporate arm of the Federal Reserve Bank system which is also a private corporation owned by financiers and internationalists.

In the federal 1995 tax table, if your income was between five and fifteen dollars, your tax is two dollars! Thus, everyone is in the federal venue—unless yearly income is under five dollars.

One percent owns ninety percent. In history, the witch burnings, the Jewish holocaust, and now the war on drugs are confiscatory approaches.

Government-corporate conglomerates are fascism; a corporation can act as the State, as the conscience of the state, over-riding the individual.

2) Government control of communications and transportation:

Freedom of speech and assembly.

FDA regulations and IRS codes are not covered by CNN.

Public-supported television is a correct balance to a media that is otherwise owned by a few in a democracy.

Control of media and spins on the truth, finance distraction via Roman bread and circus "programs" like talk shows in general, and sensational prime-time media.

3) Government ownership of factories and agriculture.

4) Government control of labor:

Union contracts are a check and balance to management. Open shop unions can nicely check any tyranny from within a union. The Fascist Party of Mussolini in the 1920s dissolved labor unions, substituting in their place "corporations" made of employers and employees who dialogued via "labor courts" (puppet courts). In 1930, The International Labor Office found that the Italian workers were the worst off in all of Europe.

5) Multi-national corporate farms, and pharmaceuticals:

A German delegate to the United Nations/ World Trade Organization Codex Alimentarius Commission has proposed that dietary supplements be limited to RDA dosages. Supplements that don't have an RDA would be illegal to sell as foods. The proposal has already taken hold in Norway, where the health food industry is being superceded by the drug companies. Via the GATT treaty, U.S. sovereignty can end in terms of health freedoms. This is all about greed, and maintaining costly treatments versus cures.

6) Abolition of all rights of inheritance:

The state will take it. In this culture, even to die can incur a debt—the average funeral cost in 1995 was at least five thousand dollars. Cremation is several hundred at least. We die in debt.

7) Disarmament of the people:

Militias that are federalized and not from the people—a police state; they are conditioning us with cop and rescue programs. Instead of militia protecting individuals and the states, armies take up arms for oil companies, or banking interests, or fast foods—grab a burger and fries on the way. Also coming our way are privatized prisons where profit, rather than the law, is the bottom line.

After the Civil War, Jim Crow laws were created to prevent black men from exercising the Second Amendment inalienable right to keep as well as bear arms. In the 1994 film *Schindler's List*, the film left out a piece of history—that Schindler later rearmed some Jews and warned them to never allow themselves to be disarmed by a government again.

Be aware that the U.S. Postal Service is a convenient way for the government to solicit citizens to register arms in order for them to be later confiscated—as are taxes on ammunition and scarce supply.

Self-defense is not vigilantism. Most U.S. states that have concealed carry laws have seen a definite decline in crime—all without wild shoot-outs.

Amendment four gives the right to privacy and security against unreasonable searches and seizures. Search warrants require probable cause.

Roadblocks condition us to give up rights, to be treated as possibly suspect without probable cause. Associative thinking may take the place of law. For example, if a person carries one-hundred-dollar bills, then the assumption is that it is drug money. The Fourth Amendment rules out neighborhood sweeps for guns, or anything else.

8) Government control of education:

Federal based schooling, or Outcome Based Education or Values Clarification, is objective. Everyone gets an A if the right answer is given—and the education system will be programmed and funded for the right answers.

Noah Webster, author of Webster's Dictionary, spoke twelve languages, including Sanskrit. He was very aware of how language changes thinking and the ability of people to communicate law. He also developed the Blue-Backed Speller (1783) knowing that the British could take sovereignty from American people who were poorly educated.

Educated jurors: jury nullification can be ruled based on the facts of the law and how the law is applied. Conscience is part of a juror's duty—a subjectivity. If all law is objective, then all driving accidents would be ruled the same whether the defendant is basically a responsible citizen who committed a tragic mistake, or a sociopathic repeater. This demonstrates the need for a jury of one's peers, and the writ of habeus corpus (literally, "the right to have the body").

The right of jurors to nullify a law has been exercised since the roots of our country. William Penn used it, and was an anarchist intent on free worship. He refused to abide by the Anglican Church in Britain. He then settled in Pennsylvania as a Quaker.

Nullification of law also helped turn over Salem witchcraft laws, and overturned Prohibition in 1933. It is the right of all to have a jury—even in drug "mandatory cases" —wherein the conscience of the jury may nullify a law. It is curious that IRS "courts" are devoid of this aspect of law. Tax courts are really bureaucracies and self-serving, rather than appealing to justice.

9) A Central Bank:

Since the American Revolution, central banks have prevailed in general in order to lessen the chaos of a confusing currency system, and debts have been no stranger to decentralized banks. In February 1791, a Bank of the United States was established designed after the Bank of England, and in 1792 a federal currency system and a mint was established. But Congress and the people refused to let it renew its charter in 1811, seeing its greed. The War of 1812 promptly ensued. In 1816, another Bank of the United States was given a federal charter. The Federalists were strong on a central government, land speculation, and an amount of ruthless capitalism. (Hamilton, a federalist, was not personally rich; he was convinced that only a small group of aristocratic, moneyed people could empower the United States.) Still, by 1811, the United States Bank was detested by farmers, the democratic party and even Congress. Its charter was not renewed. It was learned that seventy percent of the bank's stock was owned abroad.

The Constitution (Article 1, Section 8) states that: "Congress shall have power . . . to coin money, regulate

the value thereof, and of foreign coin" and to coin
money using silver and gold. And Congress may not
charge usury on its citizens. But in 1910, on Jekyll
Island, members of the Republican Party met with
elite international bankers. (This was also the year of
the Flexner Report when the Senate decided allopathy
was superior to homeopathy, and John D. Rockefeller
funded allopathy. Homeopathic schools then faded
out. Affordable health care faded out also.) In 1913 the
Federal Reserve Act was enacted—which created by
law, not by the Constitution, a private international
banking cartel—a private corporation. (In August
1914, World War I ensued: Paul Warburg, the first
chairman of the Federal Reserve Board of Governors,
was a recent immigrant from Germany whose family
banking house was the M. M. Warburg Company,
which financed Germany's war against the Allied
forces. Paul's brother, Max Warburg, headed the
German secret service. It is common knowledge that
banks have funded both sides of wars.)

The Federal Reserve banking system was created to
frustrate the "Money Trust," the large financial and
commercial interests, and to make the money supply
more even by regulating (controlling) inflation and
deflation. But this system also fell into the wrong
hands. In 1993, congressman Henry Gonzales said
that in the New York Federal Reserve District, thirty-
three percent of the medium-sized member banks and
twenty-five percent of the large member banks were
foreign-owned. Since 1916, the 1929 crash, the Great
Depression, nine recessions, and a national debt of
over six trillion paper dollars has manifested out of a
central private banking system. The average family in
1995 "owes" over 65,000 dollars to the Feds, to pay a
debt which is mostly interest.

Foreign and private banking interests are more
powerful than governments and are for their own
benefit. They control foreign customers and control
foreign relations. They operate outside constitutional

checks and balances. And amazingly, the Federal Reserve has never had an independent audit. Who profits by this debt?

The Feds have the power to use the debt of foreign nations (including our own since we borrow from them) as collateral for the printing of Federal Reserve Notes. Collateral in the U.S. can be houses, national parks, work-units (human employees). A one day sit-down could collapse the government economically. No one would buy or sell that day. Then government could be restored to the people—a scary idea if the people are not "educated" on how to be self-governing.

In 1791 Thomas Jefferson stated that "If the American People ever allow private banks to control the issue of currency, first by inflation, then by deflation, the banks and corporations that grow up around them will deprive the People of all property until their children will wake up homeless on the continent their fathers conquered."

Alexander Hamilton, a Founding Father, helped create the first central bank, with his belief that business, commerce, and the state should be preeminent, versus Jefferson's insight that the Individual is sovereign over the state. (The state must protect the individual; currency in the hands of individuals and small businessmen is where genius of invention arises, as in marketable free energy technology, but these individuals cannot compete with federally funded institutions of science or large corporations.)

Thomas Jefferson had to solicit financial help from Dutch bankers to pay the debt for the American Revolution. Today we would borrow from the Federal Reserve. One might ask, therefore, if it is not better to have the Fed, as long as most of it is homegrown.

10) A heavy progressive income tax:

During the Civil War there was an income tax, repealed in the 1870s. In 1894 was another income tax, but the Supreme Court deemed it unconstitutional.

The social security number is a contract between an individual and the corporate IRS. It is "voluntary servitude."

The IRS collects the debt on the interest for the Federal Reserve Bank—a private corporation. A seventy-seven percent tax load is projected on future generations—the progressive income tax. The idea is to repeatedly tax the same dollar and to compel private conscience to "invest" in certain ways in order to avoid more taxes. Land is viewed as investment and not a creature in its own right.

The Internal Revenue Service garners one-fifth to one-fourth of all money—double the tithe required by the medieval church.

One may go to debtor's prison if they owe the IRS!

The Fed bypasses the lawful U.S. Treasury. The only way the Treasury can get release of captive dollars is by selling bonds of equivalent amount to the Feds bonds on which all taxpayers must pay interest.

Currently, even babies are given social security numbers—they are signed into a contract while legally minors! The IRS is kidnapping our babies! Originally "not for ID purposes," now employers are bluffed into believing a social security number is a requirement for employment. It is an inalienable right to work. It is a right not to take social security benefits, and a right not to be taxed on wages. (Social Security, however, was one of the great forward advances of this compassionate nation, if having it does not contract other rights away.)

"Wages, labor and natural property cannot be taxed involuntarily" (Butlers Union Co. vs Crescent Co. 111 U.S. 746).

Labor and wages are compensation, a natural property right. Income is a profit or gain, a taxable privilege, so gambling can be taxed. The individual, unlike the corporation, must not be taxed for the mere privilege of existing.

Individuals apply for a social security number to contract into the IRS, voluntarily filing and electing to have wages called taxable income. The tyranny of the IRS compels all to comply. In the years 1913 through 1915, less than two million Americans filed income tax, for it was common knowledge that it was only for corporations and certain licensed professions. In World War II, the withholding or victory tax used patriotism to lure people in. All taxes are not bad, however. Tariffs, fees, excise taxes on corporations, and other forms of income, did in the past support the federal government. We now have huge interest payments—debts to foreign stockholders. A trillion dollars a year goes to the Feds—mostly to pay the interest. Where is it all spent? On unmarked helicopters, underground bases, UFOs, Tesla technology? Taxpayers pay over 260 billion to subsidize corporations—their special interests, federal lands use, and media time (called "corporate welfare").

The danger of the IRS is that of an Inquisition list, like Satan, an accuser of men.

You are guilty until proven innocent if there is a problem with the IRS. The Fifth Amendment is about not testifying against oneself. A century after the Salem witch trials, the founding fathers were appalled at the torture of women into confessions of practicing witchcraft. In the late 1940s and early 1950s the witch hunt for Communists in the United States added another dark chapter to American history—McCarthyism.

An IRS agent must be familiar with tax laws that cover two thousand pages of statutes and six thousand pages of regulations.

A consumptive tax is voluntary, simple, and when income tax is gone, wages go up.

The original claim was that income tax would be only on the very rich—a lure to tax everyone, except perhaps the very rich.

Early in U.S. history, the idea of lawyers being in politics was considered almost unlawful, that lawyers would blemish law. The word "attorney" means "to twist." Interestingly, George Washington called out the militia to crush the Whiskey Rebellion of 1794, which was due to a tax put on whiskey to pay the national debt.

A world currency is what the globalists want. Smart Cards can hold encyclopedic amounts of information on you. You may already apply for this. At Schipol Airport, Amsterdam, a digitized reading of the "hand"—a quick swipe of the card combined with the hand pressed against a machine reader—is all that is needed to pass immigration. The card has been issued to volunteers for free. In 1994, the INPASS card arrived for international business travelers, wherein the hand is scanned on a plate while one swipes the card to "ensure the traveler isn't a known drug lord or other undesirable," issued by the Immigration and Naturalization Service to be used at major ports of entry[1]. Fingerprints will probably be the streamlined mode in the future. It is convenient, inexpensive, and costs you only your privacy. Without it, you will not be able to buy and sell. With Smart Cards, we, employees of NAFTA, work-units travel "freely" and perhaps safer, about the world. In the Netherlands, European Identity Cards are used for employment, travel, and one can be retained twelve hours if one doesn't have one while traveling. Smart Cards open data bases to all of your files.

The U.S.A. SuperSmart card was developed by the Defense Department in conjunction with the Postal Service, the IRS and the Treasury Department. A "tessera" in Latin means "a piece of mosaic," the name given by ancient Roman conquerors to identify chits they issued to conquered peoples and slaves. Identification cards are a kind of licensure. Patrick Henry was appalled that a preacher was scourged for not taking a license to preach (freedom of speech is a right). The man had harmed no one, and was suddenly made a criminal for not having a license. Thomas Jefferson put on his visa that he was a "planter." Jefferson did not identify his being-ness as residing in a license number.

A common-law lawyer said, "Human beings walk on the land, not on paper fictions." The reason our forefathers wanted only those who owned land to vote, was not elitism, per se, but to ensure the vote came from a loyal source. They understood maritime law, or what corporate law is all about, which is by nature "off the land."

Thomas Jefferson disdained Roman civil law, which was grafted into English common law in 1760 by Lord Mansfield. This decision helped spark the American Revolution. Common law was in England 200 years before Christianity and long before the Magna Carta (1215). It contains inalienable rights, and was the basis of the Fourth and Fifth Amendments. Church law first became involved with commercial ventures when the Roman Catholic Church funded the Roman army, and so the church became involved in the civil government of Roman dictates and policies. When Roman civil law moved into England by way of commercial ventures of the mercantile church, its private law, or the conscience of the church, became a part of the economic and political fabric. (With the Council of Nicaea in A.D. 325, Emperor Constantine made Christianity the official religion of the Roman Empire. At least the persecutions of Christians ceased.) NAFTA and GATT may be a modern manifestation of what Roman law was when it touched foreign shores. Modern times are seeing mercantile entities touch lives very privately, and these are partners with government. Government and economic policies are dangerously entwined. A nation of merchants raised to a priesthood. Corporations that supercede states, merge with and dissolve free enterprise.

Corporations are fictitious legal persons distinct from their members and are created by fiat of the state. The initial British colonization of America was basically achieved via governmentally chartered trading corporations. The Italian Fascist system was based on unlimited governmental control of economic life. Hitler's National Socialist Regime was a form of the corporate state.

The history of the United States has been one of abdication of state control over corporations. In 1886 the U.S. Supreme Court declared corporations legal persons whose life, liberty and the pursuit of happiness are protected by the Fourteenth Amendment. The Fourteenth Amendment was also ratified to protect freed slaves.

(Freed slaves became subjects of the District of Columbia, rather than sovereigns over the federal government—with rights granted by the government versus inalienable rights. This is an example of when civil rights are necessary—when the dominating culture does not have the conscience of a free nation.) As late as the 1870's, states were removing charters. Directors were responsible for corporate debts and any harm caused. In 1976 the Supreme Court declared that corporations have the right of free speech and that money is a form of free speech. Corporations not only have free speech via money, but since the 1980s paid approximately seventeen percent of all federal tax versus thirty-nine percent in the 1950s. The tax load has shifted onto individuals. The danger is obvious—that individual conscience will be disempowered and the good of the corporation or the good of the state will take precedence. The individual right to "life, liberty, and the pursuit of happiness" will be viewed as a selfish thing of the past. Commercial contracts do compel the performance and conscience of the people.

It is as if Rome never fell. There was a sense of freedom in the early Roman Republic, which inspired George Washington. The later Roman Empire evolved into a system of contractual law wherein individual freedom and rights were contracted away. The Roman Empire spread, imperialistic and dictatorial, in the guise of democracy. When it fell, however, a Dark Ages followed, the earlier Republic forgotten.

My husband had a prophetic dream about the national debt, and what he calls the "graymen" who are behind these confiscations. In the dream, a woman ushered him into a long room. She said to him, "All your debts will be paid in a timely manner. The graymen's own activities will cause their demise." In the book of Revelation, the dark forces do themselves in when it seems all facets of the world order come together—the economic, the political, and the religious. The princes of darkness fall, a restoration of godliness and peace follows, a feast of jubilation. All debts are paid, and slaves freed.

The feast of jubilation was a rite of the Hebrews wherein every fifty years, property was given back to the original rightful owner. It was a way to break the spell of tyrants. Inscribed on the Liberty Bell in Philadelphia is Leviticus 25:10:

". . . and ye shall hallow the fiftieth year, and proclaim liberty throughout the land unto all the inhabitants thereof."

The rest of the passage is:

"it shall be a jubile onto you; and ye shall return every man unto his possession, and ye shall return every man unto his family,"

and

"the land shall not be sold forever: for the land is mine (God), for ye are strangers and sojourners with me" (Leviticus 25).

THE SPORT OF KINGS

No hounds have yet barked in this apple-colored dawn.
All morning the horses walk. I imagine the fox
freshly printing the hills

We pull on our boots in the oven-warmed kitchen
the tea is steeping and the porch is loud with birds

from our mounts we point to sunny cliffs where fox lived
in the days of kings

we ride and are well-groomed, pass like white fences
we stand with the hounds, the bright horn is raised
and the gun jumps.

the line easily breaks, bridles flash like beds of fish
we lope casually over the greens.

the day is pleasant, surprising our eyes, we feel capricious, perfect
like the butterflies, golden monarchs tending the southern hills

we take tea, thumb tobacco into our pipes, the creek fills with

leaves

soon someone shouts Fox, we lope toward the barking

the fox, grinning in a tree,
is smarter than we,
below is its hole, a wedge
of the pack enters

Notes:

—In the fox hunt, foxes have no tails, faces, or feet; instead, these
are referred to as "brushes," "masks" and "pads," which are cut from
the fox at death. This is perhaps an allegory to us—in that we have

identification numbers, licenses, and credit—or we are nothing. Fox hunters generally do not commune with nature, nor have they ever gone without a meal. They are the privileged class. A civilized mob. A Lord Redesdale even hunted his own children. (Foxes are not always innocent either, entering chicken coops and making a massacre of them, and then not eating a morsel.)

THE PRAIRIE BAREFOOT DEMOCRACY

I remember the prairie barefoot
democracy
the army transporting grain in tanks
angels of conception

how women felt storing the grain
how they regarded preschool kids
scuffing the dirt

you know kids are light and sound sensitive
that the army would shoot him if his feathers showed
a bird flies off to the cradling sky
bare feet looking up
"Is it the sacrificial I, not I?"

history knows it is unfulfilled
warlords take to the hills sailing
a flash crack of a long knife twist
(You are going to say its your rescuer.)

but the stars barely slip, and the foxes
fishes and white robes will be your best medicine

"For the children of this world are in their
generation wiser than the children of light."
—St. Luke (16:8)

ANGELS OF THE WHEAT

It is autumn
magnified light
he is looking down at a face
in the paper
"Another innocent has been taken."
his wife replies, "Some say
we create our own reality."
"Nothing but cold denial," he says, rising,
"Evil must be cast into a hole,
the lid twisted on."

Their voices stir
over the print
in fields of papery wind
birds cast an otherworldly blue
upon the wheat
she asks, "Don't we really die for internal reasons?"
"remember dear, the woman had no gun
and drew the thing near her."

she thinks, some cells die
so others can live
some simply fall into death easier
some are purely conscious, we don't know
how they protect themselves
one man complained of softening of the brain
a great sensitivity to light

he puts his palm on her chest
"That is a pure heart."
she takes two pencils
the drawing board stands open
she is drawing and erasing herself
an otherworldly blue
hidden beneath the wheat

Notes:

—St. Patrick detested slavery and was a rarity in speaking out against the practice. He himself was abducted from Roman Britain and bound by an Irish petty chieftain. He spent six years in isolation, tending sheep for this king. He was so forlorn that he began to believe in God and turned to prayer. Finally he escaped, and met with Irish sailors who befriended him. The sailors, starving, asked him to pray to his Christian god for help. When he did, a herd of swine appeared. Patricius became a missionary and, near the end of his life, the Irish slave trade came to a halt.

—When Rome fell, Irish monks copied all books they could get their hands on and thus preserved much Western literature that would be otherwise lost or burned in the Dark Ages that followed.

—The gradual fall of Rome was not noticed by most until the end. Taxes were high, though senators paid none. At least there was no debt to pass onto children in the sense of floating capital. The army became more like a dictatorship. Inflexible thinking and poetry that was sentimental, without originality, prevailed. With the abandonment of emperors, public buildings came into the hands of private greed. The last emperor was in 476.

—Allodial title (Noah Webster 1828 Dictionary) refers to land which is the absolute property of the owner, real estate that is not subject to rent, service, or acknowledgment of a superior. It is opposed to a feudal state. In England, there is no allodial land, all land being held by the king. (The citizens of the United States have in this century lost allodial title and reverted to a feudal-like condition in that we now pay fees to the state in the form of property taxes in exchange for the privilege of the use of the land.)

—The evil Waco event in U.S. history now joins the national disbelief and wound created by the Kennedy assassinations and Martin Luther King's.

—This author would revel in the use of reverse speech (replaying taped speech backwards) on politicians, CEOs and NASA. The reverses apparently never tell a lie. Reverse speech is the primary language. Even preverbal infants form clear sentences in the reverse tape.

(Note that dyslexia is a reverse phenomena and that optical images are first in reverse.)

The congruity between the conscious forward speech and the subconscious reverse is remarkable, with reverse speech being more metaphoric. John David Oates is a researcher and teacher on this phenomenon, which could be revolutionary in understanding the areas of speech, child development, lie detection, the mind-body relationship in disease, mental health, and schizophrenia. Reading written material backwards is not the same, however, as taping spontaneous forward speech, with its pauses, glitches, and Freudian slips. So telling and consistent is this method that John David Oates's home was burned down by persons unknown.

The Crossing

My husband, Marc, had a dream, or should we say, a visitation. In it he was feeling much distress in an environment of giant steel machines grinding and spitting out materials. After what seemed a long time of this, a woman took him to a ship that was shaped in the proportions of Noah's ark (a vesica piscis). Women in white were powering the craft by their breath, blowing into tubes, while the ship moved silently out to "some sea." One woman said, "He has so much love for you," (Marc thought, the Father in heaven?) and a black woman began chanting. Then he was approached by a young woman who noticed, "You have a block." She gently pushed something into his palate and to the back of his skull. Light began to spew forth. She sewed on him with threads of light. And then the scenery blended with another place, though he was still on "some sea in a silent ship." The zoo was a holding place for animals presently unknown to humanity. (There were white, silvery, furred camel and llama-like creatures that spread seed pods everywhere.) All the animals had white fur. But in one holding area, there was a cobra which had a steel bar and ring through its tongue. Marc was told to not let this snake out.

I wondered if this was a future Noah vision. All three brains—reptile, mammal, and light are presented. The feminine energy is the vehicle to the other side. Marc's palate is opened, and the back of the skull, the medulla oblongata, has been called the mouth of God.

The hooded snake is not yet to be released, our preparation for its transmuting power is what is laid before us now. Its magic is always to be coupled with love.

References

Chapter One: Beauty and Love

1. Matter of Heart *(film)*. 1983 C.G. Jung Institute of Los Angeles.
2. Ibid.
3. Raymond Moody, *Coming Back* (New York: Bantam, 1990), p. 14.
4. Stephen Bertman, *Doorways Through Time: The Romance of Archaeology* (Los Angeles: Jeremy P. Tarcher, Inc., 1986), p. 79.
5. William Domhoff, *The Mystique of Dreams: A Search for Utopia through Senoi Dream Theory* (Los Angeles: University of California Press, 1985), p. 28.
6. Robert Bly, *The Rag and Bone Shop of The Heart: Poems for Men* (New York: Harper Perennial, 1992), p. 319.

Chapter Two: The Divine Feminine

1. Caitlin Matthews, *Sophia: Goddess of Wisdom* (London: The Aquarium Press, 1992), p. 340.
2. Robert Bly, *American Poetry: Wildness and Domesticity* (U.S.A.: Harper Perennial, 1991), p. 67.
3. Terence Mckenna, *Food of the Gods: The Search for the Original Tree of Knowledge* (New York: Bantam, 1993), p. 141.
4. Caitlin Matthews, *Sophia: Goddess of Wisdom* (London: The Aquarium Press, 1992), p. 31.

5.   Ibid., p. 310

Chapter Three: The Divine Masculine

1.   Daniel J. Boorstin, *The Creators: A History of Heroes of the Imagination* (New York: Vintage Book, 1993), p. 54.
2.   Ibid., p. 728.
3.   Richard Hoagland, Hoagland's Mars: Vol.II, *The U.N. Briefing*, filmed in 1992.
4.   Bob Frissell, *Nothing in This Book is True, But It's Exactly How Things Are* (Berkeley: North Atlantic Books, 1994), p. 75.
5.   Samuel M. Warren, *A Compendium of Swedenborg's Theological Writings* (NY: Swedenborg Foundation, date), p. 661.
6.   Terence McKenna, *Psilocybin: Magic Mushroom Grower's Guide* (U.S.A.: OSS & O.N. Oeric, 1976), p. 14.
7.   Ibid.
8.   Ibid.
9.   Ralph Noyes, *The Crop Circle Enigma* (CA: Gateway Books, 1990), p. 173.
10.   Ibid., p. 137.

Chapter Four: The Blue Ray

1.   Stanislav Grof, *Beyond the Brain: Birth, Death, and Transcendence in Psychotherapy* (NY: State University Of New York Press, 1985), p. 271.
2.   J. J. Hurtak, *The Book of Knowledge: The Keys of Enoch* (The Academy for Future Science CA, 1987), p. 159.
3.   Ray Stanford, *Fatima Prophecy: The Message the Church Can No Longer Suppress* (NY: Ballantine Books, 1988), p. 138.
4.   Ibid., p. 162.
5.   Chet Snow, *Mass Dreams of the Future* (CA: Deep Forest Press, 1993), p. 288.
6.   Ray Stanford, *Fatima Prophecy: The Message the Church Can No Longer Suppress* (NY: Ballantine Books, 1988), p. 138.

Chapter Five: A Recipe from Lourdes

Chapter Six: The Serpent and the Sun

1. Joseph Chilton Pearce, *Evolution's End* (NY: Harper Collins, 1993), p. 190.
2. Gobi Krishna, *Kundalini for the New Age: Selected Writings of Gopi Krishna* (New York: Bantam Books, 1988), p. 3.
3. P. M. H. Atwater, *Coming Back to Life: The After-Effects of the Near-Death Experience* (NY: Ballantine Books, 1988), p. 46.
4. Sri Aurobindo, *The Adventures of Consciousness* (Pondicherry India: Sri Aurobindo Society, 1970), p. 184.
5. Ibid., p. 194.

Chapter Seven: Serpents of the Lakes

1. George C. Andrews, *Extra-Terrestrial Friends and Foes* (Georgia: Illuminet Press, 1993), p. 102.

Chapter Eight: Body Electronics of Santa Fe

Chapter Nine: Mars—the Next Eden

1. Brad Darrach and Steve Petranek, "Bringing a Dead World to Life," *Life Magazine*, May 1991, p. 32-35.
2. "New Evidence Suggests Mars has Water Under the Surface," *Los Angeles Times*, Mar. 30, 1995.
3. Arthur C. Clarke, *Profiles of the Future: An Inquiry into the Limits of the Possible* (NY: Fawcett Popular Library, 1958), p. 107.
4. Zecharia Sitchin, *Genesis Revisted* (NY: Avon Books, 1990), p. 257.
5. Richard Hoagland, "Hoagland's Mars": Vol.II, *The UN Briefing*, filmed in 1992.
6. David H. Childress and Nikola Tesla, *The Fantastic Inventions of Nikola Tesla* (U.S.A.: Adventures Unlimited, 1993), p. 282. Hoagland, "Hoagland's Mars: Vol.II", 1992.
7. Joel McClain and Norman Wootan, "The Magnetic Resonance Amplifier," *Nexus Magazine,* Feb-Mar. 1995, p. 49.

8.   Sitchin, p. 272.
         New York Times News Service, August 27, 1993.

Chapter Ten: The Star Tetrahedron and the Mer Ka Ba

1.   Robert Monroe, *Journeys Out of the Body* (N.Y: Anchor Books, 1971), p. 212.
2.   Robert Monroe, *Far Journeys* (NY: Doubleday, 1985),p. 231.

Chapter Eleven: Sacred Sites: Inner and Outer Space

1.   "No More Light Years," *Sky and Telescope*, Mar. 1994, p. 15.
2.   Associated Press, June 22, 1994.
3   Rebecca Lee, "The Jerusalem Syndrome," *The Atlantic Monthly*, May, 1995, p. 92.
4   Alice Bryant and Phyllis Galde,*The Message of the Crystal Skull: From Atlantis to the New Age* (St. Paul: Llewellyn Publishers, 1991), p. 77.
5.   Ralph Noyes, *The Crop Circle Enigma* (UK, U.S.A.: Gateway Books, 1991), p. 147.
6.   Peter Lemesurier, "Is it True What They are saying about the year 2000?" *Mountain Astrologer Magazine*, 1995.
7.   Edgar Evans Cayce, *Edgar Cayce on Atlantis* (U.S.A.: Warner Books, 1988), p. 147.
8.   Max Troth and Greg Nielson, *Pyramid Power* (NY: Warner Destiny Books, 1976), p. 196.
9.   Peter Tomkins, *Secrets of the Great Pyramid* (NY: Harper and Row, 1971), p. 57.

Chapter Twelve: The Dream Mind

1.   Matter of Heart *(film)*. 1983 C. G. Jung Institute of Los Angeles.
2.   Stephen LaBerge and Howard Rheingold, *Exploring the World of Lucid Dreaming* (NY: Ballantine Books, 1990), p. 64.

3. Chet Snow, *Mass Dreams of the Future* (CA: Deep Forest Press, 1993), p. 288.
4. Ibid., p. 293.
5. Michael Talbot, *The Holographic Universe* (U.S.A.: Harper Collins, 1993), p. 65.
6. Stephen LaBerge and Howard Rheingold, *Exploring the World of Lucid Dreaming* (NY: Ballantine Books, 1990), p. 89.
7. Ibid.
8. Morris Berman, *Coming to Our Senses* (NY: Bantam, 1989), p. 73.
9. "Unsolved Mysteries," aired May, 1993.
10. Helen Wambach, *Life Before Life* (U.S.A.: Bantam, 1929), p. 155.

Chapter Thirteen: Psychedelia and the Light Brain

1. Peter Tomkins and Christopher Bird, *The Secret Life of Plants* (NY: Harper and Row, 1973), p. ix.
2. Terence Mckenna, *Food of the Gods: The Search for the Original Tree of Knowledge* (NY: Bantam, 1992), p. 132.
3. McKenna, Terence and Dennis,*The Invisible Landscape* (U.S.A.: Seabury Press, 1975).
4. Paula Weintraub, *The OMNI Interviews* (NY: An Omni Press Book; Ticknor & Fields, 1984), p. 162.
5. Aldous Huxley, *Collected Essays* (NY: Bantam Books, 1960), p. 329.
6. Joseph Chilton Pearce, "Imagery and intelligence," *In Public Forum*, relative to melanin molecule.

Chapter Fourteen: Soul in Software

1. Linda Greg, *Sacraments of Desire* (MN: Greywolf Press, 1991). Joseph Chilton Pearce, *Magical Child* (U.S.A.: Bantam Books, 1980).
2. Ibid.
3. Marlo Morgan, *Mutant Message Downunder* (U.S.A.: MM Co., 1991), p. 62.

Chapter Fifteen: Chaos and its Forms

1. William M. Bulkeley, "Cipher Probe," *The Wall Street Journal*, 1994, April 28, vol. cxxx No. 83.
2. Ravel (album).
3. Ibid.
4. Ed Conroy, *Report on Communion* (NY: Avon Books, 1989), p. 373.
5. Joseph Chilton Pearce, *Evolution's End* (NY: Harper Collins, 1993).

Chapter Sixteen: The Universe: Sound

1. Daniel J. Boorstin, *The Creators: A History of the Heroes of the Imagination* (NY: Vintage Books, 1993), p. 162.
2. Denise Meola, *Omni Magazine,* Nov. 1994.
3. Frank Waters, *Book of the Hopi* (U.S.A.: Penguin Books, 1963), p. 4.

Chapter Seventeen: Space, Time, and God

1. Sandra Blakeslee, "The Nature of Consciousness," *The New York Times*, April 7, 1995.
2. Virginia Essene and Sheldon Nidle, *You are Becoming a Galactic Human* (CA: S. E. E. Publishing, 1994).
3. McKenna, Terence and Dennis, *The Invisible Landscape* (U.S.A.: Seabury Press, 1975).
4. Ibid.
5. Ibid.
6. Ibid.
7. Robert Monroe, *Far Journeys* (NY: Doubleday, 1985), p. 210.
8. Ibid.
9. Samuel M. Warren, *A Compendium of Swedenborg's Theological Writings* (NY: Swedenborg Foundation), p. 683.
10. Ibid., p. 676.

Chapter Eighteen: Manna and the 21st Century

1. Gopi Krishna, *Kundalini for the New Age* (NY: Bantam Books, 1988), p. 160.
2. Danah Zohar in collaboration with I. N. Marshall, *The Quantum Self : Human Nature and Consciousness as defined by the New Physics* (NY: Quill/William Morrow, 1990).

Other resources:
—David Hudson lecture at the Eclectic Viewpoint in Dallas, TX.; Feb. 1995.
—video, Superconductivity and Modern Alchemy 1995 by The Eclectic Viewpoint, Dallas, TX.
—*Nexus Magazine* (Aug./Sep. issue, 1996).

Chapter Nineteen: Alien Garden

1. David M. Jacobs, *Secret Life: Firsthand Accounts of UFO Abductions* (NY: Simon and Schuster, 1992), p. 168.
2. George C. Andrews, *Extra-Terrestrial Friends and Foes* (Georgia: Illuminet Press, 1993), p. 183
3. Whitley Strieber, *Communion* (NY: Beech Tree Books, 1987), p. 124.
4. Fred Steckling, *We Discovered Alien Bases on the Moon* (U.S.A.: G.A.F.International, 1981), p. 124.
5. "Sightings," aired 9/23/93.
6. Stuart Gordon, *The Paranormal* (London: Headline Publishing, 1992), p. 8.
7. Dale Musser, "Anatomy of a Mass UFO Abduction," *UFO Universe*, Fall 1993, p. 24.
8. C. G. Jung, *Flying Saucers: A Modern Myth of Things Seen in the Skies* (U.S.A.: Princeton University Press, 1978), p. 120. Robert Monroe, *Far Journeys* (NY: Doubleday, 1985), p. 172.

Chapter Twenty: Cetacean Garden

1. Nina Diamond, "The Dolphin Human Connection," *Mind Spirit*, June 1994, p. 37.
2. *U.S.A. Weekend*, March 1994, p. 22.

Chapter Twenty-One: Impostors

1. Jeffery Thayer, *The House of Common Law: Selected Cases Compiled on Citizenship, Natural Rights, and Sovereignty* (Santa Fe, New Mexico), p. 1179.
2. "The Committee to Restore the Constitution," *Bulletin*, May, 1994.
3. Jeffrey Thayer, "A Fiction at Law of Untold Magnitude: The Creation and Marketing of the State of New Columbia," *Perceptions*, May-June, 1995, p. 8.
4. Jeffrey Thayer, "A Fiction at Law of Untold Magnitude," *Perceptions*, Sept-Oct., 1995, p. 24.
5. Dolores Cannon, *Conversations with Nostradamus* (AR: Ozark Mountain Publishing, 1973) vol. II, III.
6. *Science Magazine*, Feb., 1995, p. 619.

Chapter Twenty-Two: Liberty

1. United States Constitution and first ten amendments.
2. *Conde Nast Traveler Magazine*, Nov., 1994, p. 68.

About the Author

Angela Menking has a Masters of Liberal Arts from St. John's College in Santa Fe, New Mexico. She also has nursing experience in both Critical Cardiac Care and Psychiatry. Ms. Menking has read her poetry at the Armory of the Arts in Santa Fe, the Center for Contemporary Arts in Santa Fe, and at Crestone, Colorado for Sri Aurobindo group during International Women's Week. She is happily married and lives in Santa Fe, New Mexico, which she truly considers the land of Enchantment; "the divine is everywhere."